THE FUTURE:

HUMAN ECOLOGY

AND

EDUCATION

by

Edward A. Sullivan

An ETC Publication
1975

C | P

Library of Congress Cataloging in Publication Data

Sullivan, Edward A.   1936-
   The future: human ecology and education.

   ([Education futures, no. 2])
   1. Education — Experimental methods.   2. Behavior
modification.   3. Biofeedback   training.   I. Title.
II. Human ecology and education. [DNLM: 1. Communication.   2. Interpersonal   relations.   3. Psychophysiology.
WL102 S949f 1974]

LB1026.S93   370.1'3   74-3249

ISBN 0-88280-010-8 $8.50

Copyright © 1975 by ETC PUBLICATIONS
18512 Pierce Terrace
Homewood, Illinois 60430

Printed in the United States of America

to
My wife Rose whose love and encouragement
has made this possible.
My children, Eddie, Paul, Mary Rose, Joe and John
who will grow and thrive in this new world.

Contents

ILLUSTRATIONS

TABLES

Preface

This book is the outgrowth of an article entitled, "Medical Biological, and Chemical Methods of Shaping the Mind," which I wrote for the April, 1972 issue of *Phi Delta Kappan*. But as I began to research the literature for a book length manuscript, I became aware of how difficult, if not impossible, it would be to include everything which has been done in the area of chemical, medical, and biological methods of shaping the mind.

As a result, certain topics were selected which seemed, in my eyes, to be the more important ones in this area of research. Other topics have not been included and it is a certainty that people will ask why they were not included. It was strictly a matter of judgement on my part.

Some of the research results are amazing. It is possible to alter man's mind in a number of ways. Yet, there remains the ethical and moral questions as to whether such alterations should be undertaken.

Research is currently in progress in which man is learning to communicate with animals. Other research is underway to determine if there is life on other planets, and if there is, to communicate with it. While this type of research is important, one has to wonder about how much better off we could be if we just learned to communicate more effectively with one another.

Would life not be much better if we all learned how to open ourselves up to others, not only to give love but also to receive it without the fear of being hurt by it?

The chemical, biological and medical means are already available for men to learn to effectively communicate with one another. We are already headed toward a system of education which will place some emphasis on teaching people to control their actions through the process of meditation and biofeedback training. Hopefully, this educative process, aided by knowledge gained from research similar to that reported in this book, will help men to communicate, to love, and to live peacefully with one another. The Era of Human Ecology will be a time in which mankind will thrive.

Cumberland, Rhode Island   Edward A. Sullivan

Chapter 1

❧❧❧❧❧❧❧❧❧❧❧❧❧❧❧❧

The Brain

Learning is a fundamental process for all of us. We all learn in a variety of ways. Central to our learning, however, is the brain.

The human brain consists of the cerebrum, the cerebellum and the brain stem. The cerebrum consists of two cerebral hemispheres and is divided into frontal, temporal, parietal and occipital regions. A longitudinal fissure divides the cerebrum into right and left halves. An interesting fact is that information received on the right side of the body is transmitted to the left side of the brain. Information received on the left side of the body is transmitted to the right side of the brain. When an object is placed in a person's left hand the representation of that object occurs in the right hemisphere of the brain. The information can then be transmitted from the right hemisphere of the brain to the left hemisphere where speech is regulated and the person can then state what the object is.

The left hemisphere is involved with analytical thinking especially language and logic. It is the left hemisphere which processes information in sequence, a necessity for logical thinking.

The right hemisphere is primarily responsible for our orientation in space, artistic talents, body awareness and recognition of faces. While each hemisphere has its own function these functions are not exclusive of each other.

Research with split-brain monkeys[1] (ones whose corpus callosum — the bundle of fibers joining the right and left hemispheres — has been severed) has shown that the two hemispheres can function simultaneously as well as independently. Split-brain monkeys have been trained to solve one learning problem with their left eye and right brain while solving a second problem with their right eye and left brain. Experimentation with split-brain people has shown that they can process more information at once than a person whose brain hemispheres have not been split.

Ornstein[2] has experimented with eye movements to confirm the specialization of the two hemispheres. Ornstein noted that when people are asked a question they will very often gaze to one side while deciding upon an answer. The type of question determines the direction of gazing. A verbal-analytical question, such as the definition of a word, produces more eye movements to the right than if the question is spatial.

Ornstein has also investigated the electroencepholagrams (EEG) of normal people as they were thinking verbally and spatially. The changes in the EEG confirm the fact that the normal human brain does have specialized thought processes. When the person is thinking verbally, the alpha rhythm in the right hemisphere increases. If the person is thinking spatially, the alpha rhythm in the left hemisphere increases. The increase of alpha wave production is a sign of decreased information processing.

No primates, other than human beings, have these specialized hemispheres which seem to be related to the evolution of language. It is thought that human beings have evolved specialized hemispheres because language and logic require sequential thought which is incompatible with the simultaneous thought that spatial orientation demands.

Dr. Michael Gazzaniga[3] of the New York University's Institute for Rehabilitative Medicine has been doing research that offers hope to many people suffering from the brain damage known as aphasia which affects language and speech. His research shows that the right side of the human brain, which was once regarded as merely a spare, seems capable of being trained to take over a communication function which was normally the property of the left side of the brain. The left side, which is the dominant half, is responsible for speech and verbalization. The right side plays a part in reasoning by putting together pieces of incoming information into patterns which it must pass on to the left side to put into speech.

THE BRAIN

FIGURE 1–1
LATERAL VIEW OF BRAIN AND SPINAL CORD

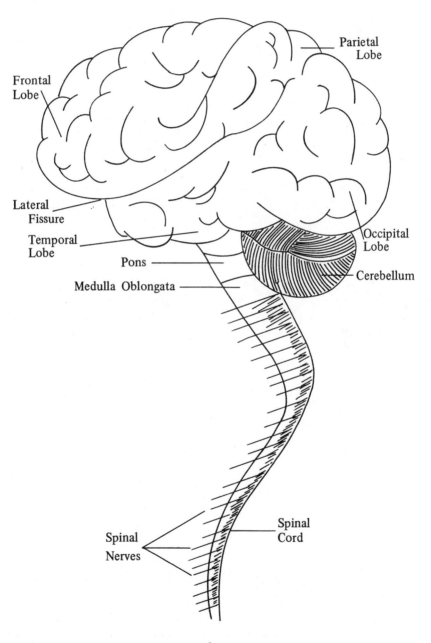

FIGURE 1–2
CROSS SECTION OF BRAIN SHOWING
CORPUS CALLOSUM

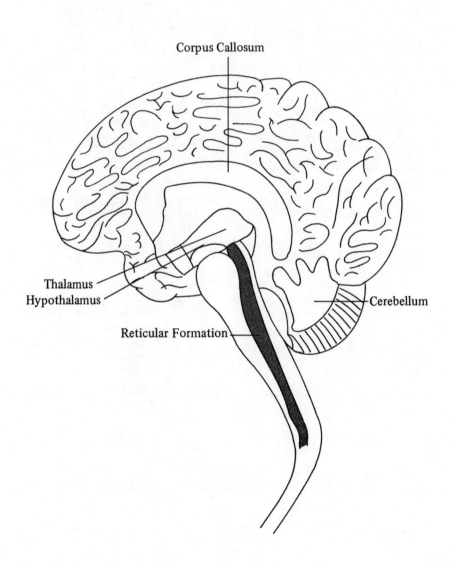

If there is some damage to the left half of the brain, such as that caused by a stroke when a blood vessel is ruptured by a clot, the person's speech and verbal comprehension processes are blocked. Attempts to restore speech to a person who suffered from such a stroke have never been successful.

Because of work done by Dr. David Premack of the University of California, in which he taught a chimpanzee to converse with him in symbolic language by indicating that two stimuli were the same, Dr. Gazzaniga thought that a stroke patient should be able to use the right side of his brain to do something comparable. The chimp was trained to place between two stimuli (apples) a particular symbol which indicated equality. Then Dr. Premack taught the chimp that when two stimuli which were not identical (an apple and a horseshoe) were placed together it should use a different symbol to indicate the inequality. The chimp had been taught to think on a very primitive level.

Work done by Allen and Beatrice Gardner[4] of the University of Nevada reinforced Dr. Gazzaniga's idea. The Gardners not only taught a chimpanzee to make the discrimination between equal and unequal symbols but also to communicate them in American Sign Language — the language used by the deaf in North America. The chimpanzee had learned a vocabulary of more than 100 words and could communicate, using Sign Language, in six word sentences.

Since the primitive mind of an ape was able to perform such communication tasks, Gazzaniga felt that stroke patients should be able to use the right side of the brain to do the same thing. Gazzaniga observed other cases in which people suffering from uncontrollable epilepsy had been operated on and the corpus callosum had been cut. The purpose was to confine the epileptic seizure to one hemisphere. The result, however, was an almost total elimination of all seizures. Such operations produced no noticeable change in the patients' temperament, personality or general intelligence.

Tests with these patients have shown that the right hemisphere does possess a certain amount of language comprehension. When the word "pencil" was flashed to the right hemisphere, in tests with these patients, they were able to pick out the pencil from a group of hidden objects with their left hand.

In still another experiment with these patients, the word "heart" was flashed across the center of the visual field with "he" to the left of the center and "art" to the right of the center. When the patients were asked to tell the word they had seen the patients would say that they had seen "art". This part of the word had been projected to the left hemisphere which is responsible for speech. When the patients were asked to point with the left hand to one of two cards to indicate the word they had seen they indicated "he." This showed that both hemispheres had simultaneously observed the parts of the word and that when given the chance to express itself the right hemisphere had prevailed over the left hemisphere.[5]

In 1971 Dr. Gazzaniga, Dr, Premack, and a graduate student began work at New York University with several patients suffering massive left hemispheric damage due to a stroke. The patients had little or no language capacity because of the stroke damage. Dr. Gazzaniga, doing as Dr. Premack had done with the chimp, placed two toy cars before the patient and inserted between them a green cutout circle. At first the patient did not comprehend what Dr. Gazzaniga was doing. But encouraged by his attitude, the patient soon performed the task by placing the green cutout circle between the two cars. Whenever the patient performed the exercise correctly, he was rewarded with a smile or a pat on the head. For one half hour each day for three weeks the patient performed the task.

The patient soon began to distinguish between similar and dissimilar objects. He was now able to communicate by relearning the most basic aspects of communication. Once the patient had accomplished this much, three-word sentences, describing simple actions, were presented. "The results were both surprising and promising," according to Dr. Gazzaniga. [6]"The residual cognitive power of severely brain-damaged people is substantial enough to build a form of lasting communication on it."

So far this work has been and still is experimental, but as a result of it, seven severely brain-damaged patients have been trained and the results are promising enough that a larger program is being developed.

Norman Geschwind[7] has indicated that in childhood the right hemisphere seems to have some capacity to take over speech functions. When there has been surgical removal of portions of the speech area to control epileptic seizures, the patients have shown milder language disorders than expected. Geschwind feels that this is probably due to the fact that the patients had been using the right hemisphere for language functions to a greater degree because they had suffered from left temporal epilepsy, involving the left side of the brain from childhood.

Doreen Kimura[8] also has shown that the right hemisphere does have the capacity to take over speech functions. Thirteen patients tested at the Montreal Neurological Institute had speech represented in the right hemisphere rather than the left.

The layer of material forming the surface of the cerebral hemisphere is the cortex. The gray matter inside the cerebrum is the basal gangli and is divided into motor, sensory, and association areas.

The motor cortex contains cells whose large axons connect with those motor neutrons of the cranial and spinal nerves that innervate skeletal muscles.

The sensory cortex is concerned with the interpretation of sensory impulses. There is a zone within the sensory cortex that sorts and records sensory information. Another zone further organizes and codes sensory information. There is still a third zone within the sensory cortex where data from other sources is combined to organize behavioral responses. An injury to the sensory cortex causes interference with the analysis of sensory stimuli and leads to disorganization of all the behavioral processes that would normally respond to these stimuli.

The association cortex occupies the greater part of the occipital, parietal, temporal and frontal lobes anterior to the motor areas. These areas are concerned with the emotional and intellectual processes involving memory, reasoning, and judgement.

The occipital association area is one of visual association. The parietal association area is concerned with the organization of thought, speech, the understanding of speech, and the ability to express common symbols in words.

The temporal association areas are believed to have an integrating function whereby we recognize body image, individuality, and continuity of the personality and self in relation to the environment.

The frontal association areas conceive and will motor acts. They also permit man to deliberate on sensory data, intellectualize and rationalize.

The frontal areas do not perform any sensory or motor functions and if these areas are injured, sensation, speech, movement, and perception are not impaired. The frontal areas serve primarily to activate the brain. Damage to this area can slow down the activating process.

The cerebellum is attached to the brain stem by bundles of nerve tissue called peduncles. The peduncles are the connecting pathways between the cerebellum and the rest of the central nervous system. The cerebellum acts as a reflex center through which coordination and refinement of muscular movement occurs. The cerebellum appears to coordinate impulses from sensory organs concerned in equilibrium with accurate muscle contractions to maintain equilibrium.

The brain stem is divided into three areas. The midbrain is the portion directly connected to the base of the brain which continues into a massive rounded structure called the pons. The pons gives way to a portion of the brain stem known as the medulla oblongata which is directly continuous with the spinal cord. The brain stem has a good deal to do with the more automatic types of muscle activity. An example of this is the muscle control necessary for us to stand up without falling. The muscular effort to stand up is taken care of without much conscious effort by automatic controls located in the brain stem.

The brain stem also controls specific functions and motions of the digestive tract as well as the respiratory rate. The respiratory rate is to some degree under voluntary control and subject to impulses from the cerebrum but interferences with the rate of respiration become difficult after a time and the brain stem takes over automatic control of the respiratory rate.

The brain tissue, as all other body tissue, is made up of cells. These cells are called neurons and are completely separated from one another by membranes. The neuron has three parts: a cell body which keeps the neuron functioning, the dendrites which form the neuron's receiving antennae and an axon, which is a single fiber extending from the cell body.

The neuron receives information through its dendrites and cell body in the form of electrochemical pulses from the other neurons. In return the neuron responds to these pulses by sending or not sending pulses of its own. Information is thus passed from one group of neurons to the next.

8

Another type of cell in the brain is the glial cell. Glial cells help to support the neurons and keep them separated from one another. Glial cells also form an insulating sheath around the axons. Multiple sclerosis can result if this sheath is destroyed. Glial cells also play a role in the feeding of neurons. The neuron does not receive its nourishment from blood vessels but has its nourishment regulated by the glia. Dr. Holger Hyden feels that the glial cells influence the neuron's manufacture of protein. If this is so, it is possible that the glial cells may have an important role in the learning and memory process.

The junction between one neuron and another is known as a synapse. Every neuron has many of these synapses. Electrical pulses, which make up the informational signals each neuron receives and acts upon, beat against the synapses. The pulses travel to the synapse and create an electrical disturbance beyond it which spreads rapidly through the membrane, through the dendrites, and through the cell body to the axon root where all outgoing pulses originate. If the disturbance at the axon root rises above a certain level, a pulse is sent down the axon.

The neuron is not stirred up by all synaptic disturbances. Some synapses actually inhibit the neuron. The inhibitory synapses seem to be as common as the excitatory ones. Without inhibitory synapses, the brain would have difficulty functioning. Inhibitory synapses sharpen the signals from sense organs by suppressing other stimuli. The inhibitory synapses also protect the brain from being overwhelmed by insignificant information. If there were not inhibitory synapses, the effect would be like an epileptic fit whenever we opened our eyes.

The simplest form of brain circuitry involves a pulse from a sensory neuron traveling to trigger motor neurons which cause muscles to contract. The motor neurons have their behavior refined and sharpened by managerial neurons which are between the sensory and motor neurons. Sensory information travels from the sensory neurons to the appropriate level of managerial neurons. At that point a command for action is determined which travels back to the appropriate motor neurons and is translated into action.

The brain possesses what seems to be a miraculous function — that is the ability to remember. It is the memory process that enables us to learn. The human body has at least four kinds of memory. The DNA (dioxyriboneucleic acid, which carries the code

FIGURE 1–3
THE SYNAPSE

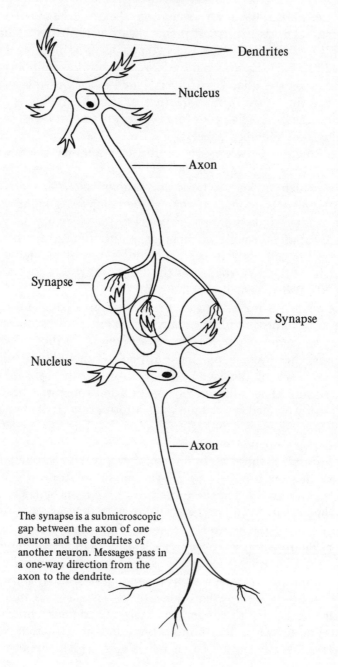

Dendrites

Nucleus

Axon

Synapse

Synapse

Nucleus

Axon

The synapse is a submicroscopic
gap between the axon of one
neuron and the dendrites of
another neuron. Messages pass in
a one-way direction from the
axon to the dendrite.

of life in each cell) has in it all the information needed to enable an individual to grow, and this information is released according to a programmed timetable. Another kind of memory is the immune system which represents a type of protective immunity. The cells in the immune system are capable of responding to any intrusion by a foreign object in the body. Once turned on, these cells will respond to an intrusion at a later time by the same object.

Memory also consists of a combination of two or more systems: sensory memory and verbal memory. It is through sensory memory that we recognize what our senses tell us. We recognize a particular taste, a smell, or the appearance of a person. To be able to explain these sensory memories, we rely upon our verbal memory system. It is the verbal memory system that allows us to store and express things in ideas and words.

The brain seems to handle verbal information on at least two levels. These two levels are short-term and long-term memory. Short-term memory can hold only a few ideas at a time, while we decide what is to be done with them. These ideas, if they are not important enough to become long-term memory, are eventually lost.

Long-term memory involves the permanent storage of an idea. If material moves from the sensory system to the short-term memory system, and is considered important enough, it will be stored in the long-term memory system.

There is a theory[9] that memories are stored in vast patterns of interconnections of millions of neurons. These patterns of interconnections are known as engrams. According to this theory, when we remember something we are refiring one of these patterns. From this theory it appears that there is no single place in the brain where memory exists, but rather that there are many places where it is to be found. This would explain how it is possible for us to remember so much as we grow older even though we lose a number of neurons every day. It would also seem to point to the idea that the hippocampus, amygdala, and thalamus, all of which have been linked with memory function, are more likely to help process rather than actually store memories.

Karl H. Pribram[10] has hypothesized that the brain uses the principle of the hologram in its memory storage process. A hologram is the recording of a scene on a photographic plate in the form of a complex interference or diffraction pattern which appears meaningless. The original image can be reconstructed if the pattern is illuminated by coherent light. The hologram is unique in its storage capacity in that every element in the original image is distributed over the entire photographic plate. When we use a regular camera and film each point on the film stores information from a single corresponding point in the photographed scene. The hologram, on the other hand, has information from the whole scene distributed to each point on the film.

The hologram, as does the brain, has a tremendous capacity to store retrievable information. The hologram can be damaged by cutting it into small pieces. Each piece will still be capable of producing the entire image when it is illuminated. The brain can also be damaged and yet the person does not necessarily lose his ability to recall the past.

Scientists are still not certain about what it is that makes long-term memory permanent. It is believed that proteins are in some way responsible because they are so important to the operation of a brain cell. If production of protein is inhibited shortly after learning, long-term memories are not made. If protein production is allowed to proceed normally after learning, the person is able to remember what he learned.

There are a number of theories to explain how protein, if it is involved, helps memories to become permanent. One theory is that the protein helps by growing new connections between the neurons involved in a particular pattern. Another theory is that protein helps by making more of the chemical needed to cross the gap at the synapse. Still another theory is that proteins could be used to build large information-containing structures within the cell body itself.

It is interesting to note the paradox of memory storage[11] by the brain which at a person's birth already contains practically all the neurons that it will ever have. It is difficult to try to explain how memory grows during learning in the absence of the reproduction of neurons. Yet, this is what does happen. Our memory grows as we learn but the number of neurons does not increase.

Reward and punishment centers in the brain play a major role in determining what we will learn. We learn sensory experiences which cause pleasure or pain. Although we know this much we still have no clear idea of the biological mechanisms of learning. It is learning and the ability to learn which distinguishes man from other primates and yet we know so little about learning.[12] As we begin to discover more about learning we should be able to bring about substantial changes for the good in the educational process, perhaps even revolutionize it.

---

[1]Robert E. Ornstein, "Right and Left Thinking," *Psychology Today*, 6: 87-92, May, 1973.

[2]*Ibid.*

[3]Michael S. Gazzaniga, "The Split Brain in Man," *Scientific American*, 217: 24-29, August, 1967.

[4]Lee Edson, "Using the Mind's 'Spare Tire'," *The New York Times*, May 7, 1972, p. 16E.

[5]Gazzaniga, *op cit.*

[6]*Ibid.*

[7]Norman Geschwind, "Language and the Brain," *Scientific American*, 226 : 76-83, April, 1972.

[8]Doreen Kimura, "The Asymmetry of the Human Brain," *Scientific American*, 228: 70-78, March, 1973.

[9]"The Mind in Action," *Life*, 71: 55-76, November 12, 1971.

[10]Karl H. Pribram, "The Brain," *Psychology Today*, 5:44-48, September, 1971. also Karl H. Pribram, *Languages of the Brain: Experimental Paradoxes and Principles in Neuropsychology.* (Englewood Cliffs, N.J.: Prentice-Hall, Inc., 1971).

[11]Karl H. Pribram, *Psychology Today, Ibid.* p. 46.

[12]For additional information on the brain and its function the following sources should be helpful:

Charles M. Butter, *Neuropsychology: The Study of Brain and Behavior.* (Belmont, Calif.: Brooks/Cole Publishing Co., 1968).

Nigel Calder, *The Mind of Man.* (New York: The Viking Press, Inc., 1971).

William Corning and Martin Balaban, *The Mind: Biological Approaches to Its Functions.* (New York: Interscience Publishers, 1968).

H. Chandler Elliott, *The Shape of Intelligence.* (New York: Charles Scribner's Sons, 1969).

THE FUTURE: HUMAN ECOLOGY AND EDUCATION

Sigmund Grollman, *The Human Body: Its Structure and Physiology*, 2nd edition. (New York: Macmillan Co., 1969).

K.S. Lashley, *Brain Mechanisms and Intelligence*. (New York: Dover Publications, Inc., 1963).

A.R. Luria, "The Functional Organization of the Brain," *Scientific American*, 222: 66-78, March, 1970.

Chapter 2

The Nervous System

In the first chapter it was mentioned that central to the learning process is the brain. The brain is a part of a system called the nervous system. The nervous system is composed of all the neurons in the body as well as the cells which provide support and nutrition for them.

The nervous system receives countless bits of information from the sensory organs and, upon reception, integrates each bit of information to determine the response which will be made by the body.

The major function of the nervous system involves the control of bodily activities. This is accomplished by control of the contraction of skeletal muscles throughout the body, control of the contraction of smooth muscles in the internal organs, and by control of the secretions of both the exocrine and endocrine glands in the body.

The nervous system is divided into a peripheral, a central, and an autonomic portion.

The peripheral nervous system consists mainly of bundles of nerve fibers which arise from the central nervous system and travel to various parts of the body. These nerve fibers are either afferent or efferent. Afferent fibers carry information from sense receptors to the central nervous system while efferent fibers carry signals which are sent to different organs from the central nervous system. Nerve cell bodies are also found in the peripheral nervous system where they form ganglia (groups of nerve cell bodies).

The peripheral nervous system contains spinal and cranial nerves as well as somatic and visceral nerve fibers. The spinal nerves emerge from the spinal cord and branch out into smaller nerves which distribute fibers to various parts of the body. Some of these fibers serve to innervate the skin while others perform a similar innervating function for the organs and tissues in the body.

The cranial nerves have their origin in the brain. They carry information from receptors located in the head and visceral organs within the body to the brain.

The somatic nerve fibers originate from cells located in the spinal cord and brain stem and are distributed to sense organs in the skin, to deep-lying tissue, to joints, and to striped muscles.

The visceral nerve fibers originate from cells located in the spinal cord and brain. They are distributed to glands and to smooth muscle areas controlled mainly through reflex action.

The visceral efferent fibers form synaptic connections in peripheral ganglia with other neurons whose fibers are sent to nerve end organs which serve to distribute impulses which activate muscle contraction and gland secretion. Collectively, the visceral efferent fibers make up the autonomic nervous system.

The autonomic nervous system is an important factor in helping an individual adjust to his environment. It helps the person by preparing him for action, for fighting or running away, for relaxing, or for digesting and excreting waste matter.

The autonomic nervous system consists of a special array of neurons which regulate body activities not generally considered under control of the will. These body activities include many functions, some of which are the heartbeat, changes in the iris, and the movement of food through the digestive tract.

In the autonomic nervous system it is possible to distinguish two channels of outflow of nervous activity. As an example, the heartbeat can be quickened or slowed down. This is done by two opposite divisions of the system — the sympathetic and parasympathetic divisions. The sympathetic division mobilizes the body for emergencies. If a person is frightened or angry or has strenuous work to do, it is the sympathetic system which causes the pupils to widen, adrenalin to be secreted, the heartbeat to be

THE NERVOUS SYSTEM

FIGURE 2–1
NERVE FIBER AND BRAIN CELLS

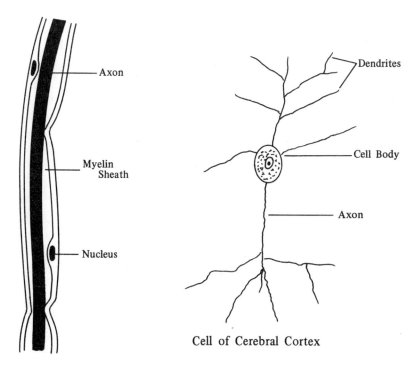

Axon

Myelin
Sheath

Nucleus

Dendrites

Cell Body

Axon

Cell of Cerebral Cortex

Nerve Fiber

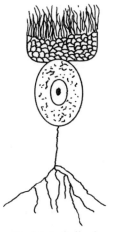

Purkinje Cell of
Cerebellar Cortex

accelerated, and the visceral blood vessels to be constricted so that blood is directed to the muscles and brain. All these events prepare the individual to deal with a trying situation.

The parasympathetic system, on the other hand, acts as a means of establishing homeostasis after the excitement has died down. Homeostasis refers to the maintenance of the internal environment within narrow limits which are conducive to normal cell function. This would mean that such factors as body temperature, blood pressure, heart rate, salt and water balance, blood sugar, and pH would be maintained at a constant level in the body. Homeostasis actually determines how efficiently the body, and especially the brain, works.

The hypothalamus, which lies under the thalamus in the fore end of the brain stem, seems to be the special control center which brings a coordinating influence to the autonomic nervous system.

The hypothalamus can affect not only the viscera but also the general body in emotional behavior. It is also possible that it affects higher levels of the brain through such visceral disorders as gastric ulcers, spastic colon, migraine headaches, and some forms of high blood pressure. The hypothalamus would seem to be an ideal area to attack these disorders by use of electrodes, surgery, and drugs.

Together with the functions previously mentioned, the hypothalamus also largely regulates the endocrine glands — small structures which discharge hormones into the blood to travel through the circulatory system.

The two endocrine glands which are especially related to the autonomic nervous system are the pituitary gland and the adrenal medulla gland.

The pituitary gland is the most complex and versatile of the endocrines. It lies directly under the hypothalamus to which it is linked by a stalk carrying hypothalamic nerve fibers and a system of blood vessels which carry a hypothalamic secretion which controls the pituitary. Pituitary hormones or hormones produced in the hypothalamus, but released in the pituitary gland, control the growth of bones, the water output of the kidneys, and other endocrine glands.

The adrenal medulla is a part of the adrenal glands which are located on each kidney. Each adrenal gland is really two different glands consisting of an outer section called the adrenal cortex and an inner core known as the adrenal medulla. The adrenal medulla secretes two closely related hormones; epinephrine and norepinephrine, which are also called adrenalin and noradrenalin respectively. Norepinephrine serves as a chemical transmitter in the sympathetic system and epinephrine plays a role in exciting smooth muscles very much like that of a chemical transmitter.

In an experiment conducted by Dr. David Shapiro[1] of the Harvard Medical School, it was demonstrated that people can be trained to exert control over functions that heretofore have been considered to be controlled by the autonomic nervous system. Dr. Shapiro trained volunteers through feedback and reinforcement to modify their blood pressure. Some volunteers had to raise their pressure while others had to decrease it. Whenever a volunteer was successful a light would be flashed on. The reward for the male volunteers, after 20 flashes, was a glimpse of a nude pinup picture. Most of the volunteers were not aware of how they controlled the flashing light and did not know what physiological function was being measured. As a result, it would seem that they had not exerted any voluntary effort to bring about the response which occurred.

Leo DiCara[2] has experimented with animals to show that supposedly involuntary responses can be learned. Curarized rats were trained to increase or decrease their heart rate in order to obtain pleasurable brain stimulation. The pleasurable stimulation occurred only during certain time periods as when a light or a tone was presented. The rats also learned to respond to one signal and not the other. The rats had demonstrated the ability to discriminate between a positive and a negative cue. In DiCara's experiments, the rats also were able to demonstrate two other properties of instrumental training which are not usually associated with visceral responses — retention and extinction. The rats showed good retention by producing the desired changes in their heart rate when they were tested three months later. Other rats also demonstrated the idea of extinction in their visceral learning. After a number of trials without any reward, the rats no longer produced the desired change in heart rate.

It is possible on the basis of these experiments to conclude that we can *teach* people with certain symptoms to get well. This possibility will be examined in more detail in the chapter on Biofeedback, chapter four.

THE FUTURE: HUMAN ECOLOGY AND EDUCATION

The central nervous system consists of the spinal cord, the medulla, the pons, the cerebellum, the mesencephalon, the diencephalon and the telencephalon.

The spinal cord is a mass of tissue which transmits sensory and motor impulses to and from the brain. Sensory signals are transmitted through the spinal nerves into each segment of the spinal cord. These signals can result in localized motor responses either in the segment of the body from which sensory information is received or in adjacent segments. All motor responses by the spinal cord are automatic and occur almost instantaneously in response to a sensory signal. They occur in specific patterns of response called reflexes.

The medulla contains cells which are involved in the regulation of such internal processes as blood pressure and respiration. It is these cells which form the nuclei from which cranial nerves emerge. Many of these nuclei are embedded in large, diffuse masses of cells and fibers called the reticular formation. The reticular formation extends throughout the brain and is involved in the regulation of movements and in the control of states of waking and sleeping.

The pons contains many of the afferent and efferent tracts which pass through the medulla. It serves as a bridge connecting the midbrain with the hindbrain. Like the medulla, the pons also contains cranial nerve nuclei and reticular formation.

The cerebellum receives sensory information from the body through fibers from the spinal cord and brain stem. Efferent fibers travel from the cerebellum to the reticular formation to control and coordinate movement.

The mesencephalon is that part of the brain which receives afferent fibers from the visual and auditory systems.

The diencephalon consists of the epithalamus, thalamus, subthalamus, and hypothalamus. The thalamus plays a part in information processing. It serves as a relay center for incoming sensory information to the cerebral cortex. Many impulses traveling from one area of the cerebral cortex to another travel by way of synapses in the thalamus. The thalamus also plays a part in reticular formation involved in sleep and waking. The subthalamus plays a part in our motor functions and the hypothalamus is involved in the regulation of internal states of the body and motivational states.

THE NERVOUS SYSTEM

The telencephalon consists of the two cerebral hemispheres and the structures within the hemispheres. Several of the structures known as the limbic system are interconnected with other parts of the cerebral hemispheres and with the thalamus and hypothalamus. The limbic system seems to be involved in emotional behavior and the learning process.

Because learning involves changes in response to a number of stimuli it is possible that memory is caused by some type of change in the nervous system. This change which results from learning could and should occur at the synapses because this appears to be the only place in the central nervous system where pathways between stimulus and response can be changed.

Jerome Kagan,[3] in a long-term study of firstborn infants, has indicated that before an infant is a year old he can activate cognitive structures to solve problems. Because of his study, Kagan feels that once the child is nine months old he has the ability to hypothesize. This makes it especially important to Kagan that developmental physiologists and anatomists search for important changes between the ages of eight months and one year. It seems reasonable to assume that the competence of the infant, as he reaches the age of nine months, should be dependent on some corresponding change in the structure and function of the central nervous system.

It is important that we find out as much as we can about the nervous system[4] because it is through increased knowledge of this system that we will be able not only to improve the learning process but also to relieve some of the physical ills caused by psychological factors. The chapters which follow develop some of the research being done in the areas of chemical, biological, and technological methods of improving the learning process.

---

[1]David Shapiro et al., "Control of Diastolic Pressure in Man by Feedback and Reinforcement," in *Biofeedback and Self-Control 1972*, (Chicago:Aldine Publishing Co., 1973) pp. 217-226.

[2]Leo V. DiCara, "Learning in the Autonomic Nervous System," *Scientific American*, 222: 30-39, January, 1970.

[3]Jerome Kagan, "Do Infants Think?" *Scientific American*, 226: 74-82, March, 1972.

4For additional information on the nervous system the sources listed in footnote 12 of chapter one as well as the following sources should be helpful:

Issac Asimov, *The Human Brain*. (Boston: Houghton Mifflin Co., 1963).

H.J. Campbell, *Correlative Physiology of the Nervous System*. (New York: Academic Press, 1965).

J.A. Deutsch and D. Deutsch, *Physiological Psychology*. (Homewood, Ill.: The Dorsey Press, 1966).

Weston D. Gardner and William A. Osburn, *Structure of the Human Body*. (Philadelphia: W.B. Saunders Co., 1967).

Arthur C. Guyton, *Structure and Function of the Nervous System*. (Philadelphia: W.B. Saunders Co., 1972).

Eric R. Kandel, "Nerve Cells and Behavior," *Scientific American*, 223: 57-70, July, 1970.

Francis Leukel, *Introduction to Physiological Psychology*. (St. Louis: The C.V. Mosby Co., 1972).

Karl H. Pribram, "The Neurophysiology of Remembering," *Scientific American*, 220: 73-86, January, 1969.

Jay M. Weiss, "Psychological Factors in Stress and Disease," *Scientific American*, 226: 104-113, June, 1972.

Chapter 3

𝕊𝕊𝕊𝕊𝕊 𝕊𝕊 𝕊𝕊𝕊 𝕊𝕊𝕊 𝕊𝕊𝕊𝕊

Electrical Stimulation
of the Brain

Until very recently not much was known about electrical stimulation of the brain (ESB). Recent research has shown that this is an area of great potential for mankind. It is also an area of great fear because of its possible misuse. The fear is that ESB will be used to manipulate the brain as a means of controlling human behavior.

It is known that the human brain consists of nerve cells which are nearly always receiving, transmitting, and discharging electrical impulses. Hans Berger, a German psychiatrist, first recorded the electrical activity of the human brain in the early 1920's. This was done by attaching electrodes to the outside of the scalp. This first electroencephalogram (EEG) was able to present only the crudest information because of the complexity of the signals given off by the brain. With the development of electronic computers, researchers have been able to sort out the signals from various areas of the brain.

A short time after Berger first recorded brain waves with his electroencephalogram, W.R. Hess, a Swiss neurophysiologist, implanted stainless steel wire electrodes in the brain of a cat. The cat was unable to feel the wire electrodes because the brain has no nerve endings in its own tissue. When Hess introduced an electrical impulse to the cat's brain by means of the electrode, the cat behaved "as if threatened by a dog." Hess wrote, "It spits, snorts or growls . . . its pupils widen . . . its ears lie back, or move back and forth to frighten the non-existing enemy."[1] It appeared that the nerve cells associated with the emotion of rage had been activated.

It had been known that there were certain areas of the brain which controlled specific functions such as hearing, speech, sight, and muscular control. Emotions at that time were not thought to be controlled in specific centers in the brain. Hess's work, however, seemed to point to the idea that there were centers within the brain which did control the various emotions. Surprisingly, even though this breakthrough had been made by Hess, a period of twenty years elapsed with practically no one working with ESB except for José Delgado.

José Delgado was born in Spain and received his medical training at Madrid University. He came to this country in 1950 to work at Yale University and has been instrumental in developing techniques for the electrical and chemical stimulation of the brain. Delgado's experiments have shown that it is possible to control psychological phenomena such as learning, conditioning, pain, and pleasure by electrical stimulation of specific areas of the brain. He has also demonstrated that social behavior can be controlled by radio stimulation of specific areas of the brain, and that human mental functions may be influenced by electrical stimulation of certain areas of the brain.

The earliest ESB involved electrodes which were placed in the brain of animals and then connected to some source of power by long wires. Animals which had electrodes implanted included cats, rats, and monkeys. Cats and rats presented no great problem in the use of ESB in this manner. But there was some problem with the monkeys who very often became curious about the wires and ended up pulling them out of their sockets. This form of ESB also required the use of an anesthetic on the animals which were to be implanted with electrodes.

In the 1950's Delgado devised a way of implanting electrodes, in which the size of the electrodes was reduced while the number of intracerebral contacts was increased. Micromanipulators made it possible to achieve a high degree of surgical accuracy in reaching selected areas of the brain and because the materials from which the electrodes were made was biologically inert, the electrodes could be left in the brain indefinitely.[2]

Damage to the brain has been found to be minimal in ESB. There is some hemorrhage but it appears to be negligible. There is also some destruction of neurons but this does not produce any detectable deficit in the brain.[3] This damage occurs when the electrodes are inserted in the brain. Insertion is accomplished by drilling a small burr hole in the skull and then guiding, by means of micromanipulators, the electrodes to their desired location in the brain. After the electrodes have been inserted, the ends of the wires are soldered to a small socket anchored to the exterior of the skull. The socket has a number of contacts each of which corresponds to an area of the brain which can be stimulated by plugging in a connector to the socket.

Brain stimulation is also possible by means of remote control. This is so because of a device called a stimoceiver, developed by Delgado. The stimoceiver permits the radio transmission and reception of electrical messages to and from the brain.

Delgado feels that stimoceivers hold promise in investigating, diagnosing, and providing therapy for cerebral disturbances in man. Some advantages of using stimoceivers in patients with temporal lobe seizures rather than other methods are:

(1) The patient is instrumented simply by plugging the stimoceiver to the head sockets.
(2) There is no disturbance of the spontaneous individual or social behavior of the patient.
(3) The subject is under continuous medical supervision and stimulations and recordings may be made day and night.
(4) Studies are carried out during spontaneous social interactions in the hospital environment without introducing factors of anxiety or stress.
(5) The brain in severely disturbed patients may be explored without confinement to a recording room.
(6) As connecting wires are not necessary there is no risk of dislodgement of electrodes during abnormal behavior.
(7) Therapeutic programmed stimulation of the brain can be prolonged for any necessary amount of time.[4]

The stimoceiver has made it possible to establish two-way radio contact between the brain of a chimpanzee and a computer. This was done by implanting a number of electrodes in the brain of a chimpanzee named Paddy. Brainwave readings were broadcast from a stimoceiver anchored on Paddy's skull to a computer. The computer, which had been programmed to detect any brainwave patterns indicative of aggressive behavior, monitored Paddy's brain waves continuously.

Whenever Paddy began to become aggressive, signals were radioed from the computer to an area of his brain which produced unpleasant sensations. Electrical stimulation of one part of the brain depended upon the production of a specific EEG pattern by another section of the brain. The computer identified the brain wave pattern and was responsible for directing the subsequent ESB. Within a period of two hours after the ESB experiment in which Paddy's brain wave pattern had at first indicated aggressive behavior, a decrease of fifty percent in such behavior had occurred. A week later the brain wave pattern indicative of aggressive behavior had all but disappeared. Paddy's behavior had changed from that of fighting to sitting peacefully in his cage.

When the computer was disconnected, it took the EEG and Paddy's behavior about two weeks to return to normal. When the experiment was repeated several times, similar results were obtained. The conclusion to be drawn from this type of experiment is that direct communication can be established between the brain and a computer, circumventing normal sensory organs, and also that automatic learning is possible by feeding signals directly into specific neuronal structures without conscious participation.[5]

Since these experiments were performed, there have been advances made in the development of stimoceivers which can now be implanted completely beneath the skin. This eliminates the need for wires leading from the brain to the stimoceiver outside the scalp. It is now possible to install stimoceivers which can be left indefinitely in the individual.

Another development which makes it possible for individuals to control symptoms of their illness by stimulating their own brain is a transistor signaling device, the intra-cranial self-stimulator (ICSS). The ICSS can be carried anywhere on a person. The ICSS transmits signals which are picked up by an electronic socket on the patient's skull. These signals are then converted into electrical impulses. It is possible by means of the ICSS for an epileptic to stimulate his brain in such a way as to prevent an epileptic seizure when he feels one coming on. The development of the ICSS could lead to new treatments for mental and nervous disorders. It should be possible for a depressed person to change his mood or for a person suffering from tension to relieve or ease the cause of the tension by stimulating that part of the brain responsible for the tension or depression.

Delgado has also been able to demonstrate how ESB may be used to control violent behavior. Delgado did this by entering a bull ring in Spain in which the bull had electrodes implanted in its brain. As the bull charged, Delgado activated a radio transmitter. The signal affected an inhibitory area of the brain, causing the bull to halt its charge at Delgado. By pushing another button on the transmitter, he caused the bull to turn and walk away. Although this demonstration of ESB raised questions about the possibility of remote-controlled behavior, Delgado stated that ESB merely sets off a train of programmed events: biochemical, thermal, enzymatic, and electrical. He further stated, "Nothing which is not already in the brain can be put there by ESB."[6]

Delgado has demonstrated that motor responses may be activated by ESB. By means of ESB Delgado has been able to cause animals to perform a number of simple movements such as frowning, flexing, chewing, turning, and twisting. He has also been able to cause animals to perform a number of more complex acts such as walking and going through a series of activities in sequence by the use of ESB.

Delgado has pointed out several limitations in the use of ESB to induce motor responses. These are 1) a lack of predictability, 2) a lack of purpose, and 3) lack of robot performance. It is not possible, when an area of the brain is stimulated for the first time, to predict what the effects will be. As stimulation occurs, the effect becomes known and predictable, but for the first stimulation the outcome is unknown. The effect of ESB is in many instances purposeless. There is usually no reason, except for ESB for the animal to move around, or yawn etc. It is possible by means of ESB to induce motivation to perform a motor act. But it is still impossible to control the sequence of movements necessary for the animal to act unless the animal has the desire to act. It is not, therefore, yet possible to develop robot performance in animals.

27

FIGURE 3–1
BRAIN WAVE PATTERN OF AN ANXIOUS PATIENT

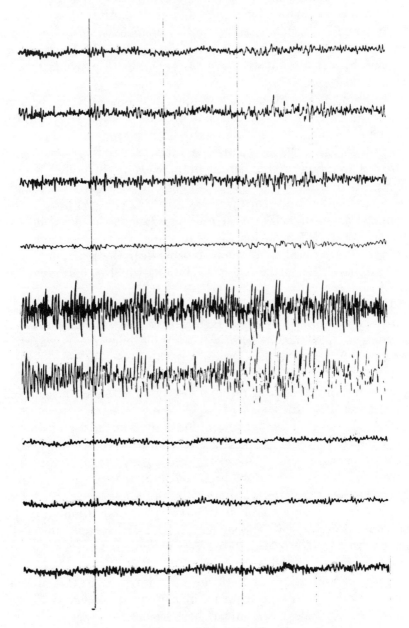

Courtesy of EEG Department, Miriam Hospital, Providence, R.I.

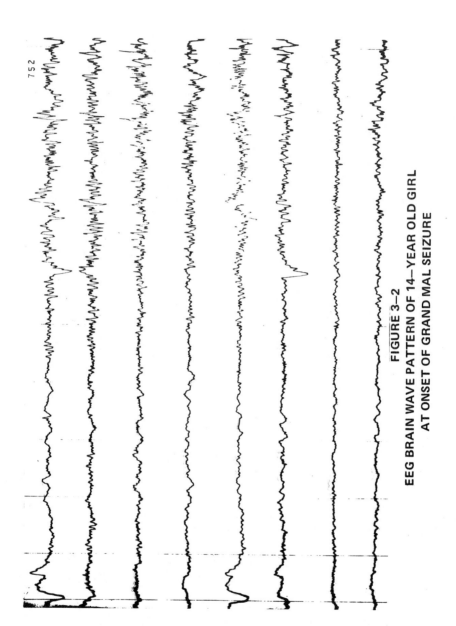

FIGURE 3–2
EEG BRAIN WAVE PATTERN OF 14–YEAR OLD GIRL
AT ONSET OF GRAND MAL SEIZURE

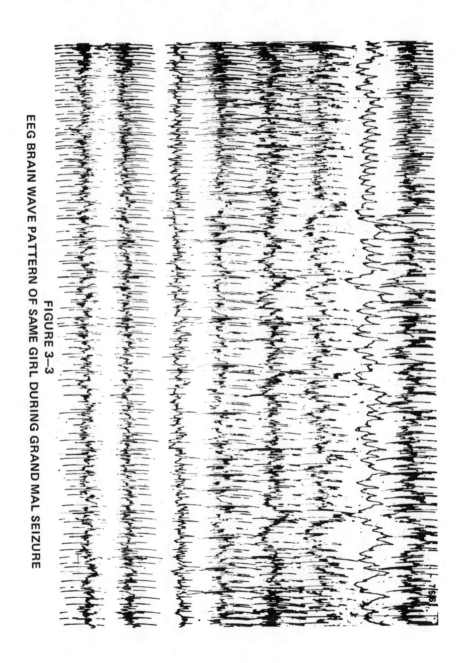

EEG BRAIN WAVE PATTERN OF SAME GIRL DURING GRAND MAL SEIZURE

FIGURE 3—3

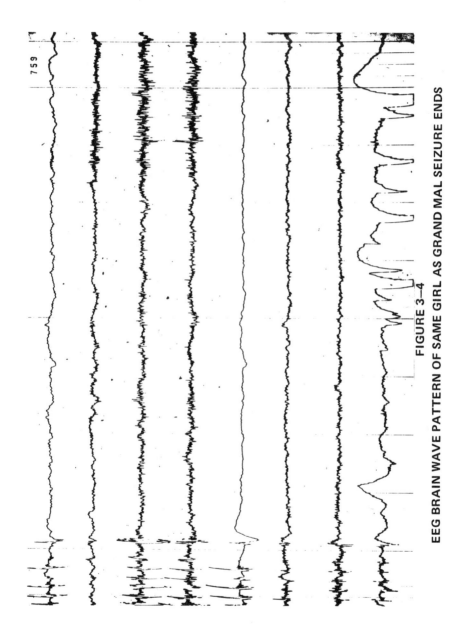

FIGURE 3–4

EEG BRAIN WAVE PATTERN OF SAME GIRL AS GRAND MAL SEIZURE ENDS

THE FUTURE: HUMAN ECOLOGY AND EDUCATION

It has been known for some time that pain and pleasure reside somewhere within the brain. The skin provides the sense receptors but the actual sensation of pain or pleasure occurs within the brain, not in the nerve endings of the skin. While this is so the brain cells, themselves, are insensitive to pain. There are no nerve endings in the brain cells. As a result, it is possible to insert electrodes into the brain and leave them there for an extended period of time without causing pain to the animal or person. Thus, ESB seems to be a viable alternative to some types of brain surgery or to institutionalization.

Persons suffering from brain disorders which result in rage and violence have had their disorders successfully treated through ESB. By means of ESB it is possible to identify the area of the brain causing the problem and also to isolate that portion of the brain for treatment.

An example of this was an attractive twenty-year-old girl whose main problem was her unpredictable and frequent attacks of rage. She had a history of epilepsy and had many grand mal attacks. Her uncontrollable rage had resulted in at least a dozen assaults on other persons. Twice she had stabbed people causing serious harm to them. Because of these events, she had been placed in a ward for the criminally insane. Electrodes were implanted in her brain to explore possible abnormalities. Because of her activity, it was impractical to confine her in the EEG room. As a result, she became one of the first human patients to receive brain stimulation through a stimoceiver. Recordings of brain wave activity as she walked through the ward showed abnormalities. Doctors were able to study these brain-wave patterns and to stimulate certain areas of the brain. By this method they were able to determine accurately the area of the brain responsible for the seizures.

Radio stimulation of a contact point in the right amygdala produced bursts of anger in the patient. One afternoon as the patient sat alone in her room playing the guitar and singing, a radio signal was sent to the stimoceiver on her skull. At the seventh second of stimulation she threw the guitar down and in a fit of rage began to beat against the wall. Stimulation of the same point produced similar violent activity on two other days. It was possible in this way to locate the specific point in the brain responsible for the violence. Once these brain cells had been identified and destroyed it was possible for the patient to lead a more normal life.

ELECTRICAL STIMULATION OF THE BRAIN

It is now possible to treat people suffering from attacks of rage and violence by using ESB by itself or in combination with surgery. It is also possible by means of ESB to induce rage and violence in an individual. Doctors can now identify the area of the brain causing the problem and can treat persons suffering from epilepsy, depression, and mental and nervous disorders by means of ESB techniques.

Delgado has also been able to demonstrate that ESB can act as a source of punishment. By stimulating hungry cats in certain areas of the brain Delgado was able to make the cats avoid food. It appeared that there were areas in the brain which correspond to the perception of pain. The results of this experimentation have been carried over to the medical field with doctors now beginning to use ESB for the relief of intractable pain.

Dr. James Olds of McGill University, after seeing the results of Delgado's study, figured that if there were pain centers in the brain there might also be pleasure centers. Olds implanted electrodes in the brains of a number of rats. In one of the rats the electrode had not been implanted exactly where Olds had wanted it to be. The electrode in this rat had entered the nerve fibers which tie together the limbic system instead of going directly to the brainstem. This rat remained in the corner of its cage where ESB occurred. If it was moved somewhere else in the cage, it would immediately return to the area where it received the ESB. The rat enjoyed the electrical stimulation in this area of the brain. A pleasure center had been found.

Dr. Olds experimented further to see what would happen if the rat were allowed to control its own ESB. This was done by installing in the rat's cage a lever which was hooked up to a battery connected to the electrode in the rat's brain. The rat learned to press the electrode with its paw, delivering an electric current to its brain and thus experiencing pleasurable stimulation. The rat enjoyed the experience so much that it gave up food, water, and sleep to press the lever and experience the pleasure. When electrodes were inserted in the same location in the brains of other rats they too enjoyed the pleasurable feeling, some of them going so far as to drop from exhaustion before stopping their lever pressing.

Since this discovery, the pleasure centers in the brains of cats, dogs, monkeys, apes, and humans, as well as other animals, have been mapped. The brain has been found to contain several separate but closely related pleasure-producing sites.

Analysis of the locations of pleasure centers in the rat has shown that 60 per cent of the brain is neutral, 35 per cent is rewarding, and only five per cent may elicit punishing effects. Because a good deal more of the brain is involved in pleasure than in pain there is hope that this predominance of the potential for pleasurable sensation can be developed into a more effective behavioral reality.[7]

Dr. C. Sem-Jacobsen of Norway conducted a study of human patients with implanted electrodes. His patients suffered from schizophrenia and Parkinson's disease. ESB at different contact points in the brain produced moods in the patients ranging from feeling good to slight euphoria to the point where the euphoria was beyond normal limits.

In a study of 23 patients who suffered from schizophrenia, one of the results of electrical stimulation of the septal region of the brain of each of the patients was euphoria. In another study a patient suffering from narcolepsia (sleep attacks) was given a stimulator and counter to record the number of times he stimulated selected points in his brain. The highest score was recorded from one point in the septal region and the patient said that pushing the button which stimulated this region made him feel good as if he were building up to a sexual climax. Needless to say the patient stayed awake when he pushed this button!

In another case, a female patient suffering from epilepsy, which could not be controlled by medication, had electrodes implanted in her right temporal lobe. Stimulation of a contact point in this area produced a pleasant sensation in the left side of the patient's body. Repetition of the stimulation made the patient so flirtatious that she expressed a desire to marry her therapist. When she was not being stimulated at this particular contact point she was much more reserved in her behavior. As a result of this and the other experiments more knowledge has been gained about the location of the pleasure centers in the human brain.

Much of Delgado's work has been done with monkeys, but its importance lies in the ability to apply what is learned about one primate — monkeys, to another primate — man. One of Delgado's most interesting experiments was his use of remote control techniques to bring about changes in the social structure of a rhesus monkey colony. These animals are social creatures and each one has a certain social rank within the colony. This rank is dependent on the aggressiveness of the monkey. The more aggressive the animal, the higher is his status. With status in a monkey colony goes the right to the best food, the best sleeping places, and the choice of available females.

Dr. Delgado's experiment involved the selection of several monkeys on various levels of social status. These monkeys had electrodes, which were connected to radio receivers strapped to their backs, implanted in their brains. By transmitting a signal to the radio receiver, Delgado was able to increase or decrease the aggressiveness of a monkey. If a high status monkey had his aggressiveness decreased the other monkeys were no longer afraid of him. He was no longer feared or respected. Once the signal was stopped, however, things changed back to normal and the monkey once again assumed his previous status position.

Dr. Delgado found that monkeys at a lower status position could be taught how to control the aggressiveness of a monkey in a higher status position. This was done by installing a switch connected to a radio transmitter just outside the monkeys' cage. It took only a few days for monkeys who were frequently attacked by a more aggressive monkey to learn to pull the switch whenever they were threatened. According to Delgado, "The old dream of an individual overpowering the strength of a dictator by remote control has come true. At least, in our monkey colonies."

It has been suggested that ESB could have still another use — this is the area of prosthesis (supplying an artificial addition to the body). It is felt that electrical signals could be applied directly to the visual cortex of the brain using a number of very small radio transmitters and receivers arranged in a grid so that a crude picture of the outside world could be represented spatially on the cortex. Experimental work on a human subject has shown that the sensation of light flashes can be produced by cortical stimulation. The picture produced in this manner is very crude because of the limitation on the number of contact points.[8]

Dr. Delgado believes that in the very near future it will be possible to have cerebral pacemakers which operate in much the same way as cardiac pacemakers. These cerebral pacemakers will treat such illnesses as epilepsy, Parkinson's disease, anxiety, fear, and violent behavior by direct stimulation of the brain. Since each of these illnesses has its own characteristic pattern of electrical activity it would be possible for a computer to monitor the brain wave pattern and once a pattern signifying the onset of one of these illnesses appeared, a radio signal could be sent which would inhibit the seizure. The person equipped with such a pacemaker would not be aware of what had happened.

Even though the medical benefits of ESB seem to be very promising there are a number of disturbing questions which arise when one talks about ESB. The question of the ethics of behavior control is raised when one mentions implanting electrodes to control violent behavior or to change an undesirable mental characteristic. Implanting electrodes is indeed a form of behavior control but how different is it from psychoanalysis, or tranquilizers, or electroshock, or a lobotomy which are forms of behavior control? Some forms of behavior control are good and ESB in this use would seem to be good. A disturbing use of ESB would be one which is foreseen by some scientists. This involves the permanent implantation of hundreds of microelectrodes in the brains of infants. The child's behavior could then be monitored and controlled by someone else with the individual becoming a robot-like adult.

Delgado is more positive in his feelings about this. He feels that ESB can help to recall memories, to awaken emotions, to disturb consciousness, to confuse sensory interpretations, and to induce fear, pleasure and changes in aggressive behavior. He does not feel that ESB can create a new personality, however.

Delgado sees ESB as being used in positive ways to control behavior unacceptable to society. Although ESB is not a teaching tool, as it does not carry specific thoughts, and it cannot be used to implant ideas in people, there is still the fear on the part of a number of people that if we can use computers to send man and satellites to the moon why would it not be possible some day to use computers to put thoughts in people's heads. Delgado feels that ESB can be used by investigators to "discover the mechanisms of anger, hate, and aggressiveness providing clues for the direction of more sociable and less cruel human beings."

Delgado sees brain stimulation as offering an experimental method for the study of the neurophysiological basis of behavior. Delgado insists that

36

True freedom will come from an understanding of how the brain works; then we will be able to control our reality. We must first start with the realization that the mind, to all intents and purposes, does not exist at birth; in some brain areas as many as 80 to 90 per cent of the neurons don't form until afterwards. Personal identity is not something we are born with. It is a combination of genetic bias, the sensory information we receive, our educational and cultural inheritance. In other words, the mind is not revealed as the child matures; it is constructed.[9]

Because of the possibilities of ESB, Delgado sees the need to develop an educational system based on the knowledge of our biological realities. This education, according to Delgado, should establish good "automatisms" in the child and, as he matures, "permit his thinking capability to evolve without being subjected to unknown forces and impulses which may overpower his rational intelligence." The possibilities of ESB are great. The ways in which it is utilized will determine to a large degree the future of man.

---

[1]Maggie Scarf, "Brain Researcher José Delgado Asks — 'What Kind of Humans Would We Like to Construct?' " *The New York Times Magazine*, (November 15, 1970). pp. 46+.

[2]José Delgado, *Physical Control of the Mind*. (New York: Harper & Row, 1969), p. 82.

[3]*Ibid*. pp. 84-85.

[4]*Ibid*, p. 91.

[5]*Ibid*. p. 93.

[6]Edward A. Sullivan, "Medical, Biological, and Chemical Methods of Shaping the Mind," *Phi Delta Kappan*, April, 1972 pp. 482-486.

[7]José Delgado, "ESB" *Psychology Today*, May, 1970, p. 51.

[8]H.S. Wolff, *Biomedical Engineering*. (New York: McGraw-Hill Book Co., 1970), p. 179.

[9]Scarf, *op. cit.* p. 170.

Chapter 4

᭝᭝᭝ ᭝᭝ ᭝᭝ ᭝᭝᭝ ᭝᭝ ᭝᭝᭝ ᭝᭝

Biofeedback Training

It has been suggested that a number of ills which plague mankind can be relieved by a single form of treatment. This treatment is known as biofeedback. Biofeedback refers to any technique which uses instrumentation to give a person immediate and continuing signals on changes in a bodily function that he is not usually conscious of. These functions include such areas as fluctuations in blood pressure, brain wave activity, or muscle tension — activities which are considered "involuntary."

Biofeedback techniques are based on the principle that certain responses are made when an organism receives information. As the organism continually receives feedback the responses are adjusted, corrected, and modified. Feedback is a vital component of learning.

A basketball player learns to shoot baskets accurately through a feedback process which involves learning to control body muscles in order to control his performance. This is accomplished by observing and acting upon the results of previous shots at the basket. This seems to be an automatic process in which not too much thought is involved.

Biofeedback is a form of feedback by means of which we are able to tune into our bodily functions and to control them. A device known as an electromyograph picks up and amplifies body signals and translates them into such easily observable signs as a flashing light, a steady tone, a beeping tone, or a tracing of a pen on a paper.

38

BIOFEEDBACK TRAINING

It was not until 1968 that the concept of biofeedback techniques became known to the public. Dr. Joseph Kamiya[1] described experiments which he had conducted in which volunteers learned to turn their brains' alpha rhythm on and off at will. This was done by means of a computer connected to an electroencephalograph which turned a sound signal on whenever alpha waves appeared in the volunteer's electroencephalogram readings. Although they couldn't explain how they did it, they soon learned to keep the tone on or off, whichever they desired, indicating that they could control the production of their alpha waves. This work, while not popularly published until 1968, had been performed in the early 1960's.

Dr. Neal E. Miller[2] and his associates at Rockefeller University have trained rats to increase and decrease their heart rates, blood pressure, intestinal contractions, and other visceral functions by means of biofeedback techniques that rewarded the correct response. As described in chapter two, Dr. Miller called this activity "instrumental learning of glandular and visceral responses." It was with this experiment that Dr. Miller challenged the belief that the individual could not consciously control physiological functions which were mediated by the autonomic nervous system. This experimentation has serious implications for the cause and cure of abnormal psychosomatic symptons and for theories of learning.

Biofeedback has been used to cure a common reading problem — subvocalization.[3] Subvocalization is the tendency to silently mouth words while reading. This procedure considerably limits the reading speed of an individual. The process of biofeedback training to cure this problem involves the placement of electrodes on the subject's neck and throat. The electrodes record the bioelectric potential generated by the movement of the vocal muscles. These potentials are amplified by an electromyograph and translated into a signal, a tone.

The subvocalization can be overcome easily. The subject, with electrodes on each side of his Adam's apple, is given a book to read silently. If he activates his speech muscles, a tone will come on. The subject is then asked to read silently, keeping the tone off as much as possible. It does not take long for the subject to keep the tone permanently off. The problem of subvocalization has thus been overcome by biofeedback.

The process of biofeedback permits an individual to monitor, by means of instrumentation, some specific inner behavior. The behavior is represented by some kind of signal which the individual is instructed to change as he observes it. When the individual changes the signal the bodily activity is changed. Biofeedback, then, involves a person changing a signal such as keeping the tone off or making the light go on. These changes indicate a modification in some bodily activity.

Dr. Herbert Benson of Harvard Medical School and Dr. David Shapiro[4] of the Harvard Psychiatry department have been successful in helping train hypertensives to lower their blood pressure by means of biofeedback. Usually for people there is no need for reward other than the success itself. In this training, however, the hypertensives receive other rewards. Whenever the patients blood pressure changes in the desired direction a beep occurs with a flash of light. For every 20 beep-flash signals, a slide is projected, which shows a scenic picture and the amount of money the patient has earned up to that time. Each projection is worth five cents and the patients are also paid five dollars for each session.

Dr. William A. Love Jr., director of the biofeedback research laboratory at Nova University, has also worked with patients suffering from hypertension. Dr. Love uses electromyograph feedback from the frontalis muscle group of the forehead to train hypertensives in deep-muscle relaxation to overcome tensions caused by environmental factors. Using Dr. Love's methods, a number of patients have successfully lowered their blood pressure.

Methods similar to those of Dr. Love have been employed with success by Dr. Thomas Budzynski and Dr. Johann Stoyva of the University of Colorado Medical Center for the relief of tension headaches. Electrodes are placed on the patient's forehead because relaxation of the frontalis muscle usually means that the scalp, neck, and upper body are relaxed as well. The patient lies on a bed wearing earphones. If the frontalis muscle contracts a tone is produced in the earphones. The greater the muscle tension the higher the pitch will be. By keeping the pitch as low as possible — through relaxation of the frontalis muscle — the patient reduces his tension headache.

Temperature feedback, a form of biofeedback, and autogenic feedback training — the use of relaxing phrases — is used at the Menninger Foundation for curing migraine headaches.[5] A patient of Dr. Elmer Green at the Menninger Foundation was being trained to control her brain waves by electroencephalographic feedback, reduce muscle tension by electromyographic feedback, and increase blood flow in her hands as measured by hand temperature. It was found that when the woman was able to raise her hand temperature 10°F in two minutes, she recovered spontaneously from her migraine. The patients were trained to measure the difference between the temperature of their index finger and the mid forehead by using a "temperature trainer." Each patient was also given a typewritten list of autogenic phrases, such as "I feel quiet," "My arms and hands are heavy and warm," "My whole body is relaxed and my hands are relaxed and warm." These phrases were to be repeated as the temperature trainer was used.

After practice for a month most of the patients no longer needed the feedback from the temperature trainer. After a year, 74 per cent of the migraine sufferers were considered improved. It appears that people suffering from migraine headaches can be assisted a good deal if they learn to regulate the blood flow between their head and hand.

Dr. S. Alexander Weinstock[6] of the Columbia University Psychology Department has also been working with people suffering from migraine headaches. His method is based on the combined techniques of self-hypnosis, the use of electromyograph biofeedback, thermal biofeedback training, and the learning of alternative responses to stressful situations.

These four methods give the patient both physiological and behavioral alternatives as a means of meeting the stress of a headache. Weinstock has worked with seven different patients with histories of headaches dating from two to thirty-five years.

The training given these patients involved a number of sessions. During the first therapy session the patient was given an example of self-induced hypnotic relaxation. This was recorded and the patient was instructed to practice this form of relaxation at least twice a day. All the patients reported that their tension and anxiety were relieved to some degree after being exposed to the hypnotic-relaxation tape.

Electromyographic biofeedback was started at the second session. Tension was measured by using the degree of relaxation of the frontalis muscle. Usually the patient was able to reduce the tension of the frontalis muscle sufficiently within 10 to 14 sessions. Once this was accomplished thermal biofeedback training was started. By practicing for between 4 to 10 sessions, each patient became able to increase his differential in temperature between his head and right index finger by 2.5 to 15°F. While this training was taking place, the patient was questioned about any external variables relating to his headaches so that anything in the environment which supported the headache behavior could be uncovered. If anything was found in this area, role-playing and training in alternative responses were instituted.

Because Dr. Weinstock has been working with this method only since 1972, it is still too soon to evaluate his results. They do appear promising though since all seven patients seem to be functioning without headaches.

Dr. Seymour Diamond, assistant professor of Neurology at the University of Chicago Medical School, and president of both the American Association for the Study of Headache and the National Migraine Foundation, has treated 200 patients using a biofeedback technique. Dr. Diamond has found that temperature training works best with young well-motivated patients who have true migraine. Temperature training does not provide help for those who have both migraine and depression or tension headache. It also is seldom of any help for anyone over 30.

Dr. Diamond has found that electromyographic feedback is very effective in the treatment of tension headaches. In his clinic, which has about 50 new headache patients a week, Dr. Diamond reports a success rate of 40 per cent with electromyographic feedback.

Dr. Bernard T. Engel, Dr. Theodore Weiss, and Dr. Eugene Bleeker [7] of the Baltimore City Hospital have used heart rate biofeedback training to help their patients with heart trouble. They have trained eight patients to control dangerous irregularities in their heartbeat by the use of mental discipline. These dangerous irregularities are known as premature ventricular contractions (PVC). There is an increased probability of sudden death with the presence of PVC.

Heart rate training took place with patients on hospital beds, hooked up to a cardiotachometer which converted their heartbeat into electrical signals. These signals were then fed into a computer, analyzed and translated into red, yellow, and green lights on a panel at the foot of the beds. Patients were directed to keep the yellow light on as much as possible. To do this, they would have to slow their heartbeats down when the red light was on or speed it up when the green light was on. By use of the lights the patients first learned to speed up their hearts and then to slow them down and finally, to keep them beating within normal limits.

The training process involved 10 sessions of 80 minutes each learning to speed up the heart beat and an equal number of sessions learning to slow it down. Once the patients had been trained, they found that they could regulate their own heartbeat without the need for artificial biofeedback. How they were able to accomplish this control could not be described by the patients. Dr. Engel feels that it should be possible to reduce the amount of time needed for this training in the future. Gay Luce and Erik Peper point out that "the training may be fundamentally tedious, and may require a long time, but unlike drugs it gives the patient a sense of mastery over his own body."[8] Five of the eight patients were able to reduce the frequency of their PVC dramatically.

Dr. George B. Whatmore of Seattle is exploring another area for the use of feedback. This is in the area of what Dr. Whatmore calls "dysponesis" — defined as misdirected or faulty effort. This misdirected or faulty effort occurs when there are errors in energy expenditure in the nervous system. Dysponesis is clinically manifested by such symptoms as fatigue, insomnia, headache, backache, hyperventilation, anxiety, depression, indigestion, impotence, frigidity, and spastic colon.

According to Dr. Whatmore:

> This kind of covert, misdirected energy expenditure can result from an unconscious bracing effort that would be appropriate to prepare for a "fight or flight" reaction to physical attack. But, if a person braces similarly in a social gathering or when he has to speak before an audience, the bracing becomes inappropriate and interferes with effective functioning. The autonomic responses it arouses are also inappropriate. Increased heart rate, elevation of blood pressure, secretion of adrenalin and other hormones, mobilization of glucose and fatty acids, and numerous other emergency responses all prepare the organism for violent muscular exertion, yet no such exertion is called for. Both the bracing and the autonomic responses interfere with normal organ function. If frequent and prolonged, they may cause tissue alterations of a pathologic nature.[9]

Dr. Whatmore feels that it is only through biofeedback training that dysponesis can be eliminated. He has found that prolonged psychoanalysis and other forms of psychotherapy have not been successful in significantly reducing dysponesis. Drugs have only served to lessen the symptoms resulting from dysponesis without altering the underlying response tendencies of the organism. The method which Dr. Whatmore has developed to eliminate dysponesis is called orthoponetics or effort training. The first step of this process involves making the patient aware of his misdirected efforts. The patient is made aware of these efforts by means of electromyographs which are attached to various parts of the body. Whenever there is any unnecessary muscle activity, it is indicated by the electromyograph. Gradually the person learns to bring these muscular responses under voluntary control. The training also involves teaching the patient to recognize and control behavior which produces these stress situations.

Dr. Whatmore has been able to follow up his work for as long as 21 years on some of his patients. He feels that he has achieved high-quality long-term results in 60 per cent of his patients, fair-quality long-term results in 20 per cent of his patients, and poor results with the remaining 20 per cent.

Electromyographic feedback is being used to restore the function of muscles crippled by strokes, spinal injuries, and other causes. The patient has an electromyograph attached to the damaged muscle and whenever he manages the least movement of the muscle being trained, a tone sounds.

Dr. Herbert F. Johnson, clinical director of the Casa Colina Hospital for Rehabilitation Medicine in Pomona, California, has been providing three 30-minute training sessions in the hospital on different days and then has the patient take and use the unit at home for two 30-minute sessions a day. In his first series of ten patients, Dr. Johnson had some who were able to walk without braces after using the unit for only a few weeks. The results have been so successful that electromyographic feedback training has become an integral part of the treatment program for stroke patients under Dr. Johnson's care.

Gardner Murphy, a psychologist, feels that biofeedback training can help people overcome the universal characteristic of self-deception. A common example of self-deception occurs when a person looks at a picture of himself and says that the picture did not come out well. The camera is blamed for the way it records a person's appearance. As we all know, the camera does not change our appearance. It merely records how we looked at a particular moment in time.

Self-deception occurs through forms of body movements that prevent unwanted information from being presented to the conscious mind. It is Murphy's belief that electrodes could be placed over muscles which are commonly associated with self-deception. By means of electromyographic feedback the person would become aware of the tightening of these muscles and be able to develop voluntary control of them. In this way he would be able to receive all the new information which flows to him.

Electromyographic biofeedback is also being used as a treatment for asthma at Denver's National Jewish Hospital and Research Center. Research psychologist Dr. Robert Kinsman heads a team which combines the deep-muscle relaxation technique, using electromyographic biofeedback, with a systematic-desensitization program. The program has not been in operation long enough for any firm conclusions to be drawn.

An associate professor of psychiatry at Boston University, Dr. Louis Vachon, has used respiratory-resistance feedback supplied by light signals which is similar to that used by Dr. Engel. Dr. Vachon found that in 28 asthmatics the average drop in respiratory resistance was about 15 per cent. This is not really enough to make the asthmatic feel any better, but it does indicate that change can be produced and that the problem now is one of producing even greater change which will allow the asthmatic some relief.

Dr. Maurice B. Sterman, chief of neuropsychology research at the Sepulveda, Californa VA Hospital is doing biofeedback research on epilepsy. His research in this area came about through the detection of a previously unrecognized electroencephalographic rhythm in cats. This rhythm which occurred only when the cat was motionless was named the sensorimotor rhythm because it was localized over the cat's sensorimotor cortex. Through experimentation Dr. Sterman learned that cats could produce this brain rhythm at will. Whenever the rhythm was produced the cat became motionless. When these same cats were exposed to a chemical possessing convulsant properties they proved to be resistant to the convulsant action of the chemical.

Dr. Sterman found that the same sensorimotor rhythm existed in man and, as with cats, was associated with motor relaxation. Dr. Sterman has been studying five epileptic patients for as long as two years. All five have shown changes in their electroencephalographic pattern in the direction of normalization. In addition to the normalization, all five patients have had fewer seizures than they had before being trained to produce the sensorimotor rhythm.

Dr. Thomas Mulholland, chief of the psychophysiology laboratory at the Bedford, Massachusetts VA Hospital is also working with five epileptics in an attempt to duplicate Dr. Sterman's findings.

Dr. Mulholland additionally is working with children who have attentional disorders, as indicated by their continuous production of alpha waves. The training involves teaching the children to suppress their alpha waves by allowing them to watch television as long as the alpha waves are suppressed. If the alpha waves appear the television shuts off and when they disappear the television is turned on again.

One of the stranger applications of biofeedback is being studied at the Claremont University Graduate School in Pomona, California. Here, men have been trained by biofeedback techniques to raise their scrotal temperature by several degrees. There is some possibility that this technique might have some possible use for contraceptive purposes.

Most of the examples of biofeedback related thus far involve electromyographic feedback. This involves some form of body-muscle training. The other form of biofeedback, brain-wave training, has some problems associated with it. One of the problems is that alpha waves are not always a sign of reduced anxiety. Some people who show no sign of alpha waves can be completely relaxed. The feeling that they must produce alpha waves to indicate that they are relaxed can be a very frustrating experience for these people.

There are four basic types of brain waves which are recorded by the electroencephalogram. These four waves include:

Beta — These are the highest frequency brain waves, associated with sense perception. As you read this you are, hopefully, in the beta state. Their frequency is 14 to 40 cycles per second.

Alpha — These waves occur from 7 to 14 cycles per second. They are associated with meditation, daydreaming, ESP, hypnosis. This is a relaxed, pleasant state of awareness.

Theta — These waves occur at 4 to 7 cycles per second. These are the waves at the borderline of sleep. This state may also be man's most creative, problem-solving range.

Delta — These waves occur at 0 to 4 cycles per second and are the brainwaves associated with deep sleep. This is the state in which newly born infants spend most of their time.

It is possible for an individual to be trained verbally to produce alpha waves without receiving biofeedback training through instrumentation. This is done by different programs, the best known of which is the Mind Control program developed by José Silva, with centers located across the country. The Mind Control course usually involves an intensive program lasting two weekends. The purpose of the program is to help people "reach a deeper, healthier level of mind."[10] One object of Mind Control is "total natural functioning" with no dependence on machines or on mental routines as occurs in biofeedback training or hypnosis.

A typical first weekend would involve the idea of Mind Over Matter. During this weekend the people in the course learn such things as sleep control, headache control, dream control, weight and habit control, and pain control. The first weekend typically also includes a memory course based on visualization and a three-finger technique for stronger programming of oneself at the alpha level. The second weekend involves ESP and psychic training.

Table 4-1
FREQUENCY OF BRAIN WAVES

Normally Unconscious		Normally Conscious	
Delta δ	Theta θ	Alpha a	Beta β
0 4	7	14	40

Cycles per Second

FIGURE 4-1
BRAIN WAVES – DELTA

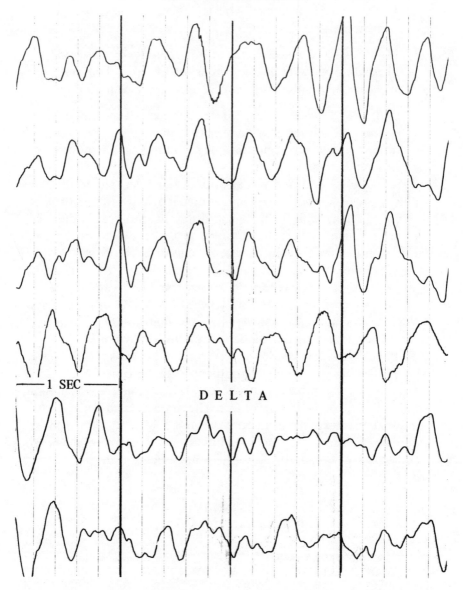

1 SEC

DELTA

The dark vertical lines represent one second time intervals. The Delta waves are those which show from 0 to 4 peaks per second.

(EEG – courtesy of Jane McGair, Miriam Hospital, Providence, R.I.)

FIGURE 4–2

BRAIN WAVES — THETA

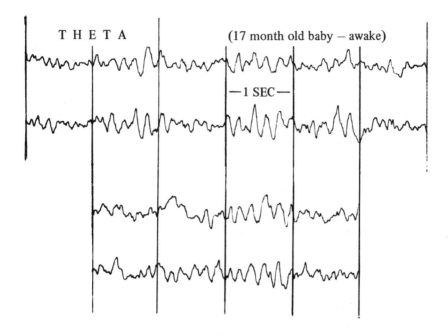

The dark vertical lines represent one second time intervals. The Theta waves are those which show from 4 to 7 peaks per second.

(EEG — courtesy of Jane McGair, Miriam Hospital, Providence, R.I.)

FIGURE 4–3
BRAIN WAVES – ALPHA

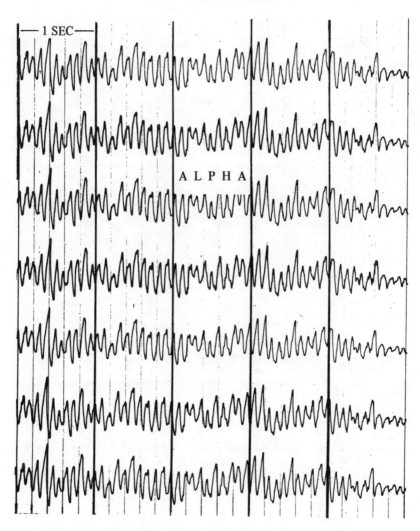

The dark vertical lines represent one second time intervals. The Alpha waves are those which show from 7 to 14 peaks per second.

(EEG – courtesy of Jane McGair, Miriam Hospital, Providence, R.I.)

FIGURE 4—4

BRAIN WAVES — BETA

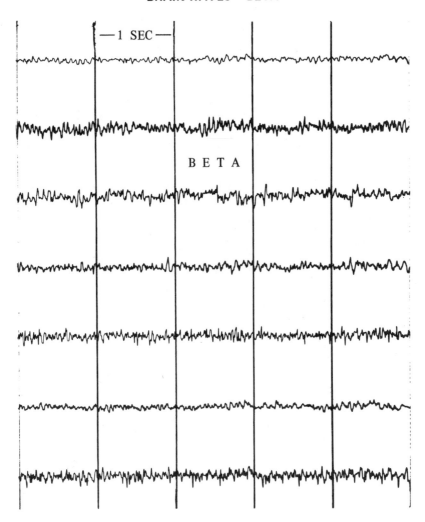

— 1 SEC —

B E T A

The dark vertical lines represent one second time intervals. The Beta waves are those which show from 14 peaks and up per second.

(EEG — courtesy of Jane McGair, Miriam Hospital, Providence, R.I.)

According to proponents of Silva Mind Control, man is able to exercise deep-seated faculties which go unused and even undetected in the beta state. The claims are also made by the Mind Control people that one can learn to relax at will, even in the middle of frantic activity, that one can summon forth great talents in art and science, and that one can project into the being of another person or that of an animal.

There are a number of scientists doing research on brain waves who are skeptical of such claims. Dr. Thomas Mulholland of the Bedford, Massachusetts VA Hospital feels that those people who report success with Mind Control share several characteristics: a tendency to look for the causes of their problems outside themselves, a readiness to find a solution to their problems, and an absence of any guilt about their own complicity in causing their own problems.[11] (This seems to describe a number of people whom we all know.)

Dr. Elmer Green of the Menninger Foundation contends that the Mind Control Program uses a hypnotic technique rather than a true biofeedback training. He also feels that unless a machine is used to identify the brain wave state for those in the program, there should be no claim made that it trains an individual for the alpha state. As indicated earlier, however, graduates of Mind Control are able to attain a high degree of alpha wave production.

A number of companies are providing Mind Control or biofeedback programs for their executives as a means of relieving tension and developing creativity. There are also several colleges which are presently offering courses in Mind Control through such varied areas as the Business, Psychology, and Religious Studies departments.

Transcendental meditation, like Mind Control, is gaining a wide following. Transcendental meditation can be defined as a method which allows the mind to be drawn automatically to the deepest and most refined level of thinking.[12]

Each person who wishes to learn transcendental meditation meets privately with a teacher and is assigned a mantra, which is a meaningless sound, but is the means by which meditation takes place. The student sits upright in a chair with his eyes closed and listens to his mantra being chanted by his teacher. The student then takes up the chant aloud and then silently. The body becomes relaxed during meditation and although the person appears to be sleeping he is still aware of what is happening around him. The training period for those wishing to learn transcendental meditation is four lessons of two hours duration.

As with Mind Control there is a good deal of skepticism on the part of scientists about the claims being made for transcendental meditation. Because of its potential as therapy for drug addicts, prisoners, and mental patients transcendental meditation is being investigated at a number of hospitals and universities across the country.

Dr. Herbert Benson and Dr. Robert K. Wallace of the Harvard Medical School have shown that during meditation a person's blood pressure is low, the heart and respiration rate is slowed, oxygen consumption is reduced and blood lactate levels, believed to be related to anxiety, decrease markedly. While all this is happening the brain wave activity which occurs is that shown by a person in a relaxed and rested state. The physiological responses found in the person meditating are also different from those that are observed in a waking, a sleeping, or a hypnotic state.[13]

Dr. Benson, who has used biofeedback techniques to slow down the heart rate and lower blood pressure, is currently training hypertensive patients to meditate to see if transcendental meditation can successfully lower blood pressure. He believes that the physiological changes observed during meditation are unique, and have not been able to be produced through biofeedback techniques.

Dr. Benson and Dr. Wallace, have found that meditation may be an effective technique in combatting drug abuse. As people practiced meditation their use of drugs decreased until most completely stopped. Most of the subjects of this study felt that transcendental meditation was instrumental in their cutting down or stopping their drug abuse.

The National Institute of Mental Health of the Department of Health, Education and Welfare awarded the International Meditation Society a grant in 1972 to train 100 secondary school teachers to teach meditation in high schools. In the Eastchester, New York school system where transcendental meditation instruction has been offered to high school students on a voluntary basis, guidance counselors report that meditators get better grades, stop using drugs, are more outgoing, and get along better with their parents and teachers.

Consideration is being given by federal prison officials and the army to training addicts to meditate. The feeling is that transcendental meditation could be of value in preventing drug abuse and combatting stress within the armed services.

Because of the biofeedback devices which have been developed, it is now possible for people to attain states that were at one time known only to practitioners of Zen and yoga. With current biofeedback devices it is possible to learn what physiological aspects are altered to attain these states. Once this is known it will be possible to train people to control the specific functions that were altered by the Zen or yoga practitioners.

An important implication for biofeedback techniques lies in the creative process. Stanley Krippner has pointed out that there is anecdotal and clinical evidence to suggest that altered states of consciousness may facilitate the creative process. Creative ability may be enhanced by enabling individuals to enter non-ordinary states of consciousness.

The alpha state has been described as a passive, contemplating type of experience.[14] Sometimes while in this state an individual can experience a oneness of himself with his surroundings. It is possible that when a person is taught to attain this state his creative powers might be increased.

It is possible that biofeedback techniques can be used to train people to develop their extra-sensory perception (ESP). ESP appears to be facilitated in altered states of consciousness. In studies which have been conducted to determine the relationship between the alpha state and ESP, results have often been contradictory. Further studies are now being conducted to determine more reliably the relationship between the alpha state and ESP.

As indicated earlier in this chapter biofeedback is being used to control drug abuse. Biofeedback seems to offer an alternative to drug abuse. It is a less dangerous method of altering one's consciousness and it also does not make the person dependent on a chemical but rather it leaves him to control his own experience.

In the medical area biofeedback places the patient in the center of the healing process. The patient becomes responsible for his own recovery. Any disease which has a specific physiological component has the potential for self-control. An ulcer patient, for example, should be able to control the acid level of his stomach by means of biofeedback processes and heal his ulcer.

Biofeedback also has potential in the area of preventive medicine. It is possible that we could develop individuals who would be able to exercise control over many of their body functions if we provided biofeedback training as a part of the school curriculum at an early age.

Perhaps the most important application of biofeedback training is in the area of education. It has been suggested that the scope of education should be broadened to include a more thorough understanding of one's bodily processes and how this knowledge enhances the self-concept. Once this is done, children should be provided with alpha and theta training so that they could more easily shift into different mental states.

Krippner[15] has suggested that a record should be kept of each pupil's brain wave patterns and overt responses. From this record instructional devices could provide an individualized program which would be based on each person's learning curve, short term memory strength, changes in consciousness while learning, special skills and disabilities, and his perceptual and cognitive styles.

If this type of program is developed, it will be possible to teach individuals to cultivate aspects of their potential which are now very often neglected.

We now have the ability to do much of what has been discussed in this chapter. Whether or not we ever actually get around to implementing the potential of biofeedback in education remains to be seen. If we do, we will be providing mankind with the opportunity to reach tremendous heights.

---

[1]Joseph Kamiya, "Conscious Control of Brain Waves," *Psychology Today,* 1:60, April, 1968.

[2]Neal E. Miller and Leo DiCara, "Instrumental Learning of Heart Rate Changes in Curarized Rats: Shaping and Specifity to Discriminative Stimulus," *Journal of Comparative and Physiological Psychology*, 63: 12-19, 1967.

[3]C. Hardyck and L. Petrinovich, "Treatment of Subvocal Speech during Reading," *Journal of Reading*, 12: 361-368+, 1969.

[4]David Shapiro, T.X. Barber et al., *Biofeedback and Self-Control 1972.* (Chicago: Aldine Publishing Co., 1973).

[5]"Biofeedback in Action," *Medical World News*, 14: 47-60, March 9, 1973.

[6]S. Alexander Weinstock, "A Tentative Procedure for the Control of Pain: Migraine and Tension Headaches," in *Biofeedback and Self-Control 1972*, pp. 510-512.

[7]Marvin Karlins and Lewis M. Andrews, *Biofeedback.* (New York: J.B. Lippincott Co., 1972) pp. 55-57.

[8]Gay Luce and Erik Peper, "Mind over Body, Mind over Mind," *The New York Times Magazine*, September 12, 1971, pp. 34-35+.

[9]"Biofeedback in Action, *Ibid.* p. 51.

[10]Robert Taylor, "The Descent into Alpha," *Boston Globe Magazine*, August 20, 1972, pp. 6-8+.

[11]Paul Langner, "Alpha Waves: Key to the Self," *Boston Sunday Globe*, March 26, 1972, p. 44.

[12]Ellen Graham, "Transcendent Trend," *The Wall Street Journal*, August 31, 1972, p. 1+.

[13]Robert K. Wallace, "Physiological Effects of Transcendental Meditation," *Science*, 167: 1751-1754, 1970.

[14]Richard Davidson and Stanley Krippner. "Biofeedback Research: The Data and Their Implications," in *Biofeedback and Self-Control 1971* ed. by Johann Stoyva, T.X. Barber et al. (Chicago: Aldine-Atherton, Inc., 1972) pp. 3-34.

[15]Stanley Krippner, "What Are Boys and Girls for?" *Journal of Learning Disabilities*, 3: 45-47, 1970.

Chapter 5

⚜⚜⚜⚜⚜⚜⚜⚜⚜⚜⚜⚜⚜⚜⚜

The Biology of Human Violence

As we study the history of mankind we can see that violence has been present in every society in every age. We seem, as a society, to abhor violence but we will not hesitate to use violence to prevent what we consider to be another form of violence against ourselves. If we are threatened by another individual or if a nation is threatened by another nation, then, to the individual or to the nation threatened, violence appears to be a viable alternative for protection. The determination as to whether violence is good or bad depends upon the perspective of the viewer. In this chapter we will be discussing violent behavior as behavior which violates the rights of another person. We will also look at some of the theories which attempt to explain the reasons for violent behavior.

In the United States, the national rate for such violent crimes as criminal homicide, forcible rape, aggravated assault, and robbery has risen considerably in the last ten years.[1] While the reported crime rate is high, there is reason to believe that there is probably just as much violent criminal activity which is not reported. This general belief is due to a lack of respect for the ability of the police to solve the crime, lack of time to report a crime to the police, lack of knowledge as to how to report the crime, and probably the most important reason — fear of reprisal.

It is interesting to note that although violent crime occurs in all areas, it is predominantly a phenomenon of large cities in the

57

United States. The larger cities which contain about 17 per cent of the total population contribute about 45 per cent of the total reported major violent crimes.[2]

Violent crime in the cities is committed mainly by young males between the ages of fifteen and twenty-four who live in the lower-income areas. The area in which the greatest number of violent crimes occur in a ghetto slum area. Contrary to what many middle class whites believe, it is not the whites who make up the majority of victims of violent crime. For victims of violent crime generally have the same characteristics as those who commit the crimes. They are generally poor, black male youths. In the case of rape, the victim tends strongly to be younger women rather than older women and of the same race as the rapist.[3]

Dr. Alvin F. Poussaint, a Black psychiatrist, in an essay entitled "Why Blacks Killed Blacks," has restated the theory that it is the economic and social frustrations of a sharply segregated society and the pressures of poverty that lead to violence — violence which is directed at the first available target.

Dr. Kenneth Clark, a psychologist and president of the Metropolitan Applied Research Center, has also endorsed the theory that frustration is responsible for much of the Black violence which is directed at other Blacks.

In studies done by Clifford Shaw and Henry McKay of Chicago from 1900 through the 1960's it was found that the poorest and most disorganized communities have always had the highest delinquency rates. This included each group of ghetto dwellers — the Germans, Polish, Irish and Italians, and most recently the Blacks and Puerto Ricans. As each group moved out of the ghetto, its delinquency rate declined. Once the frustration and pressure of poverty had been relieved, delinquency was reduced. This fact points to the need to relieve such frustration and pressure for today's ghetto dwellers.

Violent crime, with its offenders and victims, is most often found in urban areas characterized by:

    low income
    physical deterioration
    dependency
    racial and ethnic concentrations
    broken homes

working mothers
low levels of education and vocational skills
high unemployment
high proportion of single males
overcrowded and substandard housing
high rate of tuberculosis and infant mortality
low rate of home ownership or single-family dwellings
mixed land use
high population density[4]

It has also been shown in studies that young boys become delinquent and exhibit violent behavior when they come from families where consistent parental affection is lacking. If the father is frequently absent from the home, the boy will have trouble identifying with a stable positive male image. The same will hold true if the father is erratic in his behavior, unfair in his discipline, or treated without respect by others. If there is a stable integrated family life, the boy can find this to be a strong counteractive force against delinquency and violence.

Violent people are also very often frustrated people. Many are frustrated by failure and escape by means of alcohol, drugs, suicide, or mental illness. Others take out their frustrations in the form of aggression. One of the places in which frustration breeds is in the slum ghetto. The frustration is often expressed in violence. Violence becomes accepted as a part of everyday life because the necessary conditions for the development of violent subcultures exist in our cities today.

In acts of violence, persons are disposed to inflate weak or shaken egos by taking some aggressive action against others. The act of violence is closely related to feelings of inferiority. As a result, violence is often associated with incompetence and sexual violence always means sexual incompetence.[5]

As evidence of this, all one need do is read of such mass murders, made even grimmer by the sexual perversion and sadism involved, as were allegedly committed in the Houston area by Dean Corll and his two accomplices. In August, 1973, in a number of burial sites in Texas, twenty-seven bodies of young boys were discovered, victims of the largest mass murder in the recent history of the United States.

TABLE 5 - 1
INDEX OF CRIME, UNITED STATES, 1960-1972

Population	Total Crime Index	Violent Crime	Property Crime	Murder non-neg man-slau'ter	Forcible Rape	Robbery	Aggra-vated Assault
No. of offenses							
1960 179,323,175	2,019,600	285,980	1,733,600	9,030	17,030	107,340	152,580
1961 182,953,000	2,087,500	286,880	1,800,600	8,660	17,060	106,170	154,990
1962 185,822,000	2,219,000	298,900	1,920,100	8,460	17,390	110,340	162,710
1963 188,531,000	2,441,900	314,230	2,127,700	8,560	17,490	115,930	172,250
1964 191,334,000	2,761,050	361,050	2,400,600	9,280	21,230	129,780	200,760
1965 193,818,000	2,937,400	384,020	2,553,400	9,880	23,200	138,040	212,900
1966 195,857,000	3,272,200	426,470	2,845,700	10,950	25,590	157,250	232,680
1967 197,864,000	3,811,300	495,740	3,315,600	12,130	27,380	201,970	254,260
1968 199,861,000	4,477,200	590,160	3,887,000	13,690	31,380	261,620	283,470
1969 201,921,000	5,013,100	656,520	4,356,600	14,640	36,840	297,460	307,580
1970 203,184,772	5,581,200	732,940	4,848,300	15,860	37,650	348,240	331,190
1971 206,256,000	5,995,200	810,020	5,185,200	17,630	41,890	385,910	364,600
1972 208,232,000	5,891,900	828,150	5,063,800	18,520	46,430	374,560	388,650
Percent Change 1960-1972	+191.7	+189.6	+192.1	+105.0	+172.6	+248.9	+154.7
Rate per 100,000 inhabitants							
1960	1,126.2	159.5	966.7	5.0	9.5	59.9	85.1
1961	1,141.0	156.8	984.2	4.7	9.3	58.0	84.7
1962	1,194.2	160.9	1,033.3	4.6	9.4	59.4	87.6
1963	1,295.2	166.7	1,128.6	4.5	9.3	61.5	91.4
1964	1,443.4	188.7	1,254.7	4.9	11.1	67.8	104.9
1965	1,515.5	198.1	1,317.4	5.1	12.0	71.2	109.8
1966	1,670.7	217.7	1,452.9	5.6	13.1	80.3	118.8
1967	1,926.2	250.5	1,675.7	6.1	13.8	102.1	128.5
1968	2,240.2	295.3	1,944.9	6.8	15.7	130.9	141.8
1969	2,482.7	325.1	2,157.6	7.3	18.2	147.3	152.3
1970	2,746.9	360.7	2,386.1	7.8	18.5	171.4	163.0
1971	2,906.7	392.7	2,514.0	8.5	20.3	187.1	176.8
1972	2,829.5	397.7	2,431.8	8.9	22.3	179.9	186.6
Percent Change 1960-1972	+151.2	+149.3	+151.6	+ 78.0	+134.7	+200.3	+119.3

Adapted from FBI Uniform Crime Reports, 1972

FIGURE 5–1
CRIMES OF VIOLENCE 1960–1972

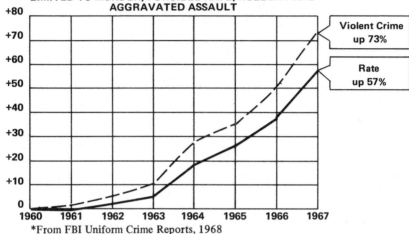

CRIMES OF VIOLENCE *
1960 – 1967
PERCENT CHANGE OVER 1960
LIMITED TO MURDER, FORCIBLE RAPE, ROBBERY AND AGGRAVATED ASSAULT

*From FBI Uniform Crime Reports, 1968

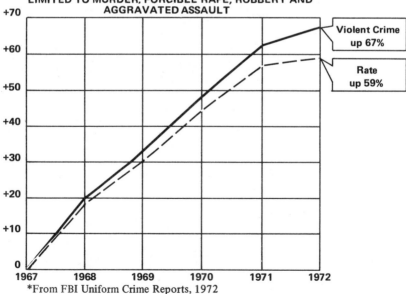

CRIMES OF VIOLENCE *
1967 – 1972
PERCENT CHANGE OVER 1967
LIMITED TO MURDER, FORCIBLE RAPE, ROBBERY AND AGGRAVATED ASSAULT

*From FBI Uniform Crime Reports, 1972

FIGURE 5–2
MURDER 1960–1972

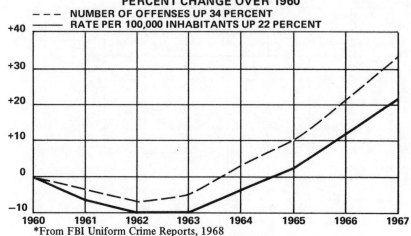

MURDER*
1960 – 1967
PERCENT CHANGE OVER 1960
– – – NUMBER OF OFFENSES UP 34 PERCENT
——— RATE PER 100,000 INHABITANTS UP 22 PERCENT

*From FBI Uniform Crime Reports, 1968

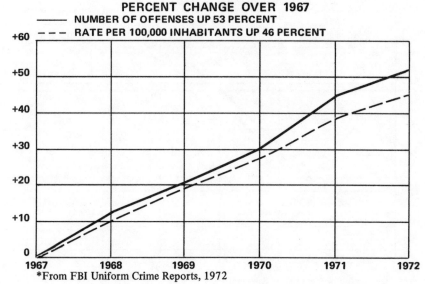

MURDER*
1967 – 1972
PERCENT CHANGE OVER 1967
——— NUMBER OF OFFENSES UP 53 PERCENT
– – – RATE PER 100,000 INHABITANTS UP 46 PERCENT

*From FBI Uniform Crime Reports, 1972

FIGURE 5–3
AGGRAVATED ASSAULT 1960–1972

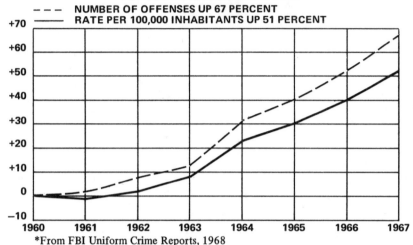

AGGRAVATED ASSAULT *
1960 – 1967
PERCENT CHANGE OVER 1960
– – – NUMBER OF OFFENSES UP 67 PERCENT
——— RATE PER 100,000 INHABITANTS UP 51 PERCENT

*From FBI Uniform Crime Reports, 1968

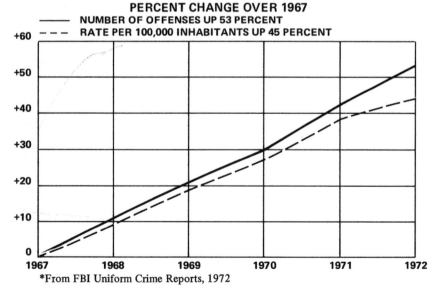

AGGRAVATED ASSAULT *
1967 – 1972
PERCENT CHANGE OVER 1967
——— NUMBER OF OFFENSES UP 53 PERCENT
– – – RATE PER 100,000 INHABITANTS UP 45 PERCENT

*From FBI Uniform Crime Reports, 1972

63

FIGURE 5–4
FORCIBLE RAPE 1960–1972

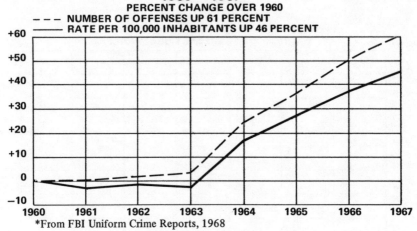

**FORCIBLE RAPE *
1960 – 1967**
PERCENT CHANGE OVER 1960
– – – NUMBER OF OFFENSES UP 61 PERCENT
——— RATE PER 100,000 INHABITANTS UP 46 PERCENT

*From FBI Uniform Crime Reports, 1968

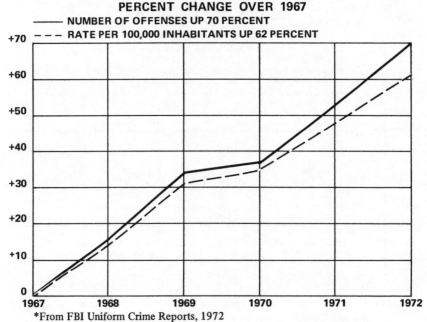

**FORCIBLE RAPE *
1967 – 1972**
PERCENT CHANGE OVER 1967
——— NUMBER OF OFFENSES UP 70 PERCENT
– – – RATE PER 100,000 INHABITANTS UP 62 PERCENT

*From FBI Uniform Crime Reports, 1972

THE BIOLOGY OF HUMAN VIOLENCE

Violence has been classified into three main groupings by Hartogs and Artzt.[6] These groupings include organized violence which is patterned and deliberate, spontaneous violence which is unplanned violence set off by a unique chemistry of external and internal conditions, and pathological violence which occurs when the person who commits the violence is not legally sane.

There are several theories which attempt to explain violent behavior. One theory states that violence is a biological phenomenon resulting from the gene structure. Another theory proposes that man is not born with tendencies to violent behavior but that he learns how to act violently because of his surroundings. Still another theory holds that we have centers for violent behavior in our brain.

The idea that the gene structure might be involved in violent behavior first came to public view in 1965. In that year Patricia A. Jacobs of Western General Hospital in Edinburgh published her findings based on a study of 197 mentally abnormal inmates undergoing treatment for their dangerous, violent conduct. She found that 3.5 per cent of the inmates had the XYY chromosomal constitution even though this type occurs only in 1.3 out of 1,000 live births.[7] Since publication of Jacobs' report, a number of other studies have been done which confirm her studies.

It is the extra Y chromosome which increases the chances of violence. The person with a normal XY chromosomal constitution does not seem to be as prone to violence as the individual with the XYY makeup. It would seem that the XYY chromosomal constitution is a result of failure of the sex chromosomes to separate normally.

In normal development an X sperm plus an X ovum produce a normal female, or a Y sperm plus an X ovum produce a normal male. If the sperm has not divided properly the XYY male can develop as a result of a YY sperm fertilization of an X ovum.

The people with the XYY chromosomal constitution are usually taller than six feet in height. They are usually dull with an I.Q. range between 80 and 95. They seem to have a high degree of brain dysfunction as evidenced by abnormal electroencephalographic recordings, and a high incidence of epileptic conditions.

Because of the great frequency with which XYY individuals commit acts of violence, it appears that in a number of cases the

65

additional Y chromosome may exert some influence in the onset of violent behavior.[8] How much influence, if any, we do not really know. The XYY individual does not necessarily have to be a violent person. There is a wide spectrum of behavioral possibilities ranging from totally normal to violently aggressive which can characterize persons of XYY makeup. What is known is that the XYY chromosomal makeup is associated with violent behavior in a large number of individuals. It is entirely possible, however, that the violent behavior of the XYY type could be caused by brain dysfunction which is a characteristic of this particular type of individual rather than because of the extra Y chromosome.

Another theory as to why people are violent is that the violent behavior is learned in response to a person's surroundings. We have all seen children learning through imitation or reward and punishment. There is a theory that children learn violence in the same way. If a child has a parent or parents who are brutal, he has a model of violent behavior. When he becomes an adult, and even as a child, violence can become an accepted part of his life because he has learned by imitation.

This theory is further reinforced by studies which show the effect on children of viewing violence on television and in films. A study by Albert Bandura, a psychologist, shows that nursery school children will readily imitate violent behavior shown by an aggressive model on what appears to be a television screen. When the aggressive model wins, he is imitated more frequently than when he is punished. It did not matter to the children whether the behavior they imitated was bad as long as it was the behavior of a model who won.[9] If we watch the cartoons and other television programs that our children see in the course of a week we would see that there is, indeed, a tremendous amount of violence portrayed.

A further aspect of the theory that violent behavior is learned is that violence is a means of coping with frustration. This can be the frustration of relative deprivation or the frustration of powerlessness. If one does not have the opportunities, or rights, or goods which he believes he is entitled to, his frustration, because of relative deprivation, can easily lead to violence as was seen in the rioting which occurred in the summers during the 1960's.

It is when people feel that conditions can be changed but see that they are not being changed that violence occurs. People seem to be able to tolerate a great deal of injustice as long as they have no hope. It is not despair or hopelessness which breeds violence. It is the hypocrisy of a system which shows people what can and should be theirs, but which never allows them to attain it, which breeds violence. It is not so much the injustice of a system but the hypocrisy of the system which causes people to become violent.[10]

Powerlessness is a very severe form of frustration. A person who feels that he is controlled by everyone around him develops this feeling of powerlessness. The only way he can exert power himself is by turning to violence.[11] This person is typified by the profile of a "typical American assassin" drawn up by the National Commission on the Causes and Prevention of Violence in 1969. The characteristics proved to be quite accurate in describing Arthur Bremer who attempted to assassinate Alabama governor George C. Wallace during his 1972 presidential campaign.

> According to the report: The next assassin to strike at a President or presidential candidate will be a white male with a short — slight build . . . and he will choose a handgun as a weapon. He will be withdrawn, a loner, no girl friends, either unmarried or a failure at marriage . . . He will have been unable to work steadily in the year prior to the assassination, and when he works it is at menial or low level tasks.[12]

The report of the Commission further describes American assassins as "deranged, self-appointed saviors." This description written three years prior to his assassination attempt accurately describes Arthur Bremer. Bremer is white, five feet, six inches tall and his weapon was a .38 caliber revolver. He had had an unsuccessful romance with a 16-year old girl and had considered killing himself because of his failure with her. At the time of the assassination attempt Bremer, who was described as a loner by those who knew him, was unemployed having worked previously as a part-time janitor and bus boy.

Dr. David Abrahamsen, a New York psychiatrist further describes assassins as having a very low level of frustration. Because he feels threatened he has to act out his impulses whenever there is the possibility of doing so.

THE FUTURE: HUMAN ECOLOGY AND EDUCATION

Dr. Roger Birkman, an industrial psychologist in Houston and Dr. Blair Justice of the Texas School of Public Health have developed a system for detecting violence-prone people before they become violent. The system was tested on 173 inmates of the Texas Department of Corrections. Seventy-eight of the inmates had committed nonviolent crimes and ninety-five had records of violent crime. They were measured on self-image and social perception scales as well as on an interest inventory and an intelligence test. The results of these tests were then fed into a computer which classified the men as violent or non-violent without knowing their records. The computer classification matched the violence records of the individuals tested.

The results showed that both the violent and non-violent inmates had a poor self-image and less of a balanced mixture of personality traits than 1,445 men outside of prison whose test scores were compared with the prisoners.

Non-violent men were more self-critical and self-conscious and viewed themselves as more sociable. They were also able to vent hostility by working with their hands while the violent directed their hostility at other people.

The violent saw themselves as individualists at the same time that the non-violent wanted a well-ordered life with a set routine. The violent were also interested in social service jobs, art or music and viewed other people as materialistic.

It is expected that these profiles will be used to draw up suitable rehabilitation programs for the inmates. Such programs would be used to encourage constructive interests while avoiding situations that might encourage violent tendencies.

Birkman has hopes that the tests can also be used to classify school children to spot potentially violent people. By use of his tests, he feels that it will also be possible to determine a child's course of study based not only on his I.Q. but also on his emotional needs. There is a good deal of concern that this type of computer assisted testing could lead to a *1984* system of living. Birkman has denied this by saying that his tests do not accumulate detailed case histories which might be damaging to an individual.

A powerful force for violent behavior, which seems at first glance to be out of line, is obedience to legitimate authority. That obedience to legitimate authority can produce violent behavior was demonstrated very vividly by Stanley Milgram in a series of experiments which supposedly measured the effect of punishment on learning. The experiments involved two people — one who acted as a teacher and another who was Milgram's assistant who acted as student. The "teacher" was instructed to give progressively more severe shocks to the "student" because of errors he made in a learning task. What the "teacher" did not know was that no shocks were actually administered.

Milgram found that the more remote the victim was psychologically, the larger the proportion of "teachers" who gave the maximum shock of 480 volts. If the "student" was in an adjoining room and protested only once by pounding on the wall, two-thirds of the "teachers" gave the maximum shock in response to the experimenter's urging. If the "student" was in plain sight and struggling and screaming one-third of the "teachers" still gave the maximum shock at the experimenter's urging.[13] The "teachers" were simply obeying the experimenter who represented authority. They apparently felt that it was permissible to do something which was against their conscience as long as someone in authority ordered them to do it. The same thing can happen to soldiers entering a village in enemy territory. Conscience is often put aside by an order from a commanding officer to destroy the enemy. The enemy can, at that point, be the elderly, the women and the children and the soldier fires because he was ordered to. Obedience becomes the force leading to violence.

Konrad Lorenz and Robert Ardrey do not believe that violent acts of man are learned. Lorenz argues that aggression in man is innate. He takes the position that there is a "fighting instinct in beast and man which is directed against members of the same species."[14]

Robert Ardrey also claims that aggression is an innate drive in humans as well as animals. According to Ardrey, this aggressive drive in man stems from strong territorial imperatives which govern the world of both men and animals. Ardrey sees man's evolution and development as having been determined by an inborn aggressive instinct, which motivated man to develop deadly weapons because, unlike animals, he possessed none of his own.[15]

In contrast to this idea is Marvin Wolfgang's declaration that:

We find no physiological evidence of any spontaneous
stimuli for fighting arising with the body of a normal
organism . . . We are therefore directed to the external
social environment as the area where the causative key to
aggression must presently be found.16

Some other interesting theories as to what makes people violent
have been proposed. Dr. Augustus F. Kinzel, a teacher of
psychiatry at the Columbia University College of Physicians and
Surgeons, has found that men imprisoned for crimes of violence are
much more sensitive to the physical closeness of others than
prisoners convicted of property crimes. Those prisoners with a
history of violence had a body buffer zone which was almost four
times larger than those who did not have a history of violent
behavior. Violent individuals perceived nonthreatening intrusion as
an attack in a number of cases.

Dr. Edward T. Hall, an anthropologist at the Illinois Institute of
Technology has done research on the needs for physical separation
shown by people brought up in different cultures. As but one
example, the body buffer zone Italians require is much less than
that for Americans. As a result of his studies, Dr. Hall feels that
physical crowding may be a direct cause of crimes of violence.

On the other hand, Dr. Francis Defeudis, a research psychiatrist
at the Indiana University School of Medicine, has found that social
isolation changes the biochemistry of the brain and nervous system
temporarily but profoundly. Social isolation — lack of contact with
others — reduces the body's ability to produce natural inhibitors
which suppress anti-social and psychotic behavior. The experiment
by Dr. Defeudis was performed with a large number of mice, but
Dr. Defeudis believes that the results are also applicable to man
because of the similarity between the biochemistry of men and
mice. In Dr. Defeudis' experiment mice, which had been isolated,
reacted violently toward other mice when they were removed from
isolation and placed with the other mice.

In other research, Dr. Arnold L. Lieber, a senior resident in
psychiatry at the University of Miami Medical School, conducted a
study which showed the relationship between phases of the moon
and the murder rate in Dade County.

Using computer programs Dr. Lieber and Dr. Carolyn R. Sherin of the University of Miami analyzed nearly 1,900 murders that occurred between 1956 and 1970. According to the data the county's murder rate began to rise about 24 hours before the full moon, reached a peak at full moon, then dropped back before climbing to a secondary peak at the new moon. During the period of maximum tidal force, when the moon and sun are lined up together in such a way as to exert the maximal gravitational force on the earth, there seemed to be an even greater increase in violent crime.

Since the body is made up of essentially the same minerals in the same proportion as the earth's surface, Dr. Lieber feels that the effect of the moon's gravitational pull on humans, though small, may be enough to touch off emotional instability in people who are borderline cases. This instability, according to Dr. Lieber, is reflected in the increased murder rate at the time of the full and new moon.

Dr. K.E. Moyer, a Psychology professor at Carnegie Mellon University in Pittsburgh, has presented a physiological model of human aggression. His basic premise for such a model is that "the brain contains inborn neutral systems that, when active in the presence of particular stimuli, result in aggressive behavior toward those stimuli."[17]

There are many examples of the presence of such neutral systems in man.[18] By means of electrical stimulation of the brain, verbal and physical aggression has been produced in a number of people. This would indicate the presence of some form of neural system which can be turned on to produce violence. Electrical stimulation of the brain, specifically the amygdala, produces aggressive behavior. A tumor in this region of the brain can also be instrumental in causing violent behavior. A well-known example of this is the case of the University of Texas sniper, Charles Whitman, who shot and killed 14 people while wounding 31 more in August, 1966. Charles Whitman, when he committed this act of violence, had a large tumor growing near his amygdala.

According to Moyer, a person's aggressiveness depends upon the state of the neural systems that govern aggressive behavior. If the systems are active and appropriate stimuli are present, then, the person will act aggressively. It is the interaction between a person's environment and his nervous system which is the key to Moyer's model of human aggression.[19]

Moyer includes a number of factors which influence the sensitivity of the aggressive system. The first of these factors is heredity. Moyer believes that just as we inherit a tendency toward epilepsy, we also inherit whatever aggressive tendencies we have.

Another factor, according to Moyer, is input from other neural systems in the brain. If these other systems are stimulated, they can increase or restrict aggressive behavior.

A third factor which influences the sensitivity of the aggressive system is any change in the blood chemistry. These changes, due mainly to change in the steroid hormone levels, can produce aggressive behavior. J.H. Morton[20] found that hostility and irritability are components of premenstrual tension. In a survey of 249 female prisoners, Morton found that 62 per cent of their violent crimes were committed during the premenstrual week and only two per cent of the violent crimes were committed at the end of the menstrual period.

The last factor affecting the threshold for aggressive behavior, according to Moyer, is learning. We can teach people how to be aggressive or how to inhibit their aggression by the use of reward and punishment. It is possible to develop or learn a habit for aggressive behavior. It seems evident from these factors that man's aggressiveness is due to some interaction of biological factors and learning.

A great deal of experimentation has shown that it is possible to bring about a physiological reduction of aggression in animals by means of brain lesions. These lesions take the form of the removal of the temporal lobes. Similar operations have been performed on humans and, while reducing aggressive behavior, have produced a number of other problems. These problems include loss of recognition of people, increased sexual activity, serious memory deficiencies and bulimia, which is an abnormal increase in the sensation of hunger. Lesions of the temporal lobe have been used to control epilepsy which cannot be controlled by the use of drugs. With these patients there has been a beneficial side effect — a reduction of aggressive behavior.

Brain lesions in the amygdala have shown great promise in the reduction of aggressive behavior in humans. None of the problems, associated with temporal lobe lesions, accompany lesions in the amygdala. The only result is the one desired — a reduction of aggressive behavior.

Besides brain lesions it is also possible to control aggressive behavior by the use of electrical stimulation of the brain. Electrical stimulation of the brain causes the neural systems which send inhibitory fibers to the aggression systems to be activated. As mentioned in chapter three, José Delgado has implanted electrodes in monkeys, chimpanzees, and bulls and has reduced their aggressive behavior by electrical stimulation of the brain. In one of Delgado's experiments electrical stimulation of the brain of an aggressive monkey was done by using a radio transmitter. When the button for the transmitter was placed inside a cage of monkeys one of the monkeys learned to press the button whenever the aggressive monkey made a threatening gesture. One monkey was able to control the aggressive behavior of another one by pushing a button. The aggressive monkey, because of the electrical stimulation of his brain, calmed down and became less aggressive.[21]

It is also possible to elicit aggressive behavior in natural non-killers by means of electrical stimulation of various sites in the brain. Rats have been electrically stimulated at various sites in the hypothalamus and the result of such stimulation was that they killed mice in the same cage.[22] The electrical stimulation can produce either an aggressive or calming attitude, depending upon where it occurs in the brain.

In man, stimulation of various areas of the brain has a calming effect. It is now possible to implant electrodes, attached to a stimoceiver, in an area of the brain which would inhibit aggression. As long as the individual remained within range of the transmitter sending out the impulses to the stimoceiver, he would be able to lead a normal life, free of the fear of acting too aggressively. It is very possible that electrical stimulation of the brain can provide a long-term control for violent behavior.

Treatment of some disorders has shown that chemical factors in the blood stream may be responsible for violent behavior. Female hormones have been used to control aggression in man in a limited number of cases.[23] As previously mentioned in this chapter, women in the week prior to menstruation commit a significantly higher percentage of violent crimes than at any other time in their menstrual cycle. A number of women repeat that they are more tense, irritable, and hostile during the week prior to menstruation. The tension of this premenstrual week seems to be associated with a drop in the progesterone level in the blood. Women who take birth control pills containing progesterone are much less irritable at this time than women who do not have their progesterone level maintained.

Another example of a chemical factor in the blood stream which may be responsible for violent behavior occurs in the illness hypoglycemia. People who have hypoglycemia — low blood sugar — in a number of cases also show aggressive behavior as well as hyperirritability and unsocial or antisocial behavior. Low blood sugar has also been implicated as a causal factor in hostility and crime. Hypoglycemia and its effects can be treated by altering the chemistry of the blood either through diet or through the use of adrenocortical steroids.[24]

It is also possible through the use of drugs to reduce aggressive behavior. Dilantin is such a drug which was used for some time to control the seizures of epileptics. It is now being used to control hostility and aggressiveness in non-epileptics.

Another drug which reduces aggressive behavior is diphenylhydantoin (DPH). The Dreyfus Medical Foundation has spent more than $7 million on DPH research. One of the projects sponsored by the Foundation involved prisoners at the Worcester, Massachusetts House of Correction. Eleven prisoners, jailed for violent crimes and subject to frequent violent action, were given DPH. Their behavior immediately improved. DPH had the same effect when given to delinquent boys and neurotic patients. They became less anxious, less angry, and less irritable after taking DPH.

Dr. Frank Ervin, director of the Stanley Cobb Laboratories of Psychiatric Research at the Massachusetts General Hospital and Dr. Vernon Mark, director of neurosurgical services at Boston City Hospital, believe that the role of brain damage may be seriously underestimated as a cause of violence.[25]

Kenefick and Glaser in an earlier study pointed to the same idea:

> ... After almost half a century of a relative neglect of the possibility of biologic defect being important in at least a few cases of criminality, we are probably ready to re-assess the problem. For example ... poor people are exposed to

the possibility of brain damage around the time of birth to a much greater degree than middle-class individuals. Also . . . this is a good deal less likely to be diagnosed when the patient is poor. Most individuals with mild brain damage do not, of course, become criminals . . . However the combination of (a) lower-class culture which tends to permit a certain impulsivity to normals and does not frown upon physical violence as much as middle-class culture; (b) muscularity, when present, and (c) a tendency to labile responses, emotionally and physically, over and above those seen in normals — all this makes some brain-damaged youngsters likely perpetrators of an "assault" and, under certain conditions, murder.[26]

Recent studies which seem to back up Mark and Ervin point to the fact that alcohol, which has been associated with a significant percentage of violent crimes, has specific harmful effects on the portion of animal brains dealing with impulse control.

Mark and Ervin feel that the brain and the environment are equal factors in producing behavior. Their experience with several hundred violent patients has convinced them that a large percentage of repeatedly violent people suffer from some form of epilepsy or brain defects that make them act the way they do. Violence is a characteristic of people with temporal lobe epilepsy. A study of prisoners with histories of violent behavior showed that temporal lobe epilepsy was found 10 times as often among them than it was found among the general population. According to Dr. Mark, epilepsy is not a disease, but a symptom of electrical disorganization within the brain.

The brain disorders which lead to violent behavior can be caused by a number of factors such as genetic defects, severe blows to the head, malnutrition in expectant mothers or young children, temporary shut off of the brain's blood supply during birth or as a result of a stroke or an accident, alcohol and amphetamines. According to Dr. Ervin, chronic amphetamine use is associated with temporal lobe-like psychoses which can lead to violent behavior.

Mark and Ervin have used surgery as a means of treating the brain disorders causing violent behavior. An operation, known as

75

stereotactic surgery, has been used to control violent behavior. Stereotactic surgery is a technique which uses a special instrument to guide thin metal electrodes to precise points deep within the brain. Doctors can spot brain cells which are misfiring by recording brain waves from the electrodes and stimulating various cells to observe their response. When the cells which are misfiring are detected, they can be selectively destroyed by heat which is radiated through the electrodes. This method destroys far less brain tissue than a lobectomy — the removal of the front part of the temporal lobe — which has been the traditional surgical treatment for patients with severe temporal lobe epilepsy. Another advantage to stereotactic surgery is that the electrodes can be left inside the brain for some time to monitor or even halt attacks of violence. This is done by stimulating the proper electrodes by remote control.

The stereotactic surgery performed by Dr. Mark involved the amygdala, which is an almond-shaped nucleus in front of the temporal lobes with important connections to many portions of the limbic system. It exerts an important modulating influence over emotional activity. Eleven patients of Dr. Mark have had tissue destroyed in the amygdalotomy procedure. Of this group only six have been followed for more than three years since surgery. Of the six, two are strikingly better and two are considerably improved in regards to seizures and attacks of rage. The two other patients who were psychotic before the operation have remained psychotic.

Dr. Ervin feels that the ultimate control in the prevention of brain misfunction is self-control. Ervin hopes that some day it will be possible to teach victims of brain damage to use the proper nerve circuits to turn off seizures by means of some form of biofeedback. According to Ervin, "We can already demonstrate that even in a brain-damaged individual with recurring violent episodes, neural mechanisms remain intact which turn off destructive behavior. Our mission is to make these mechanisms available to the individual if he can learn how to use them."[27]

Ervin is devising a 30-minute screening test for violence-prone individuals. It is his belief that it is of top priority to develop a way to identify individuals whose brains are likely to predispose them to commit violence. He feels that a battery of tests such as he is developing should be administered to all who come before the courts accused of a violent crime, repeated traffic offenders, and those involved in repeated assaults against others.

When a similar proposal to screen all children between the ages 6 and 8 was made in early 1970 by a New York physician to the White House there was a considerable outcry against it.

There is an even greater outcry at the present time over the type of surgery performed by Dr. Mark and others. This surgery, known as psychosurgery, is defined as surgery on various parts of the brain which show no demonstrable disease to change behavior or relieve tensions and anxieties. Dr. Peter Breggin, a psychiatrist in Washington, D.C. contends that at least 1000 patients in the United States have been recent victims of psychosurgery which he defines as destruction or mutilation of healthy parts of the brain in order to affect the individual's emotional and personal conduct.

Dr. Breggin is particularly concerned about Dr. Mark's amygdalotomy because the amygdala is the major "moderator and switchboard for the entire limbic and hence for all emotions and drives, and even for all higher level activities through its connections to the frontal lobes."[28]

Dr. Mark has an antithetical concern that the attacks on the use of surgery to treat brain disease associated with assaultive behavior will divert attention from the genuine issues raised by the application of a medical approach to the social problem of violence.

In July, 1973, a three judge panel in Detroit ruled that psychosurgery to alter violent behavior could not be performed on persons being held involuntarily in mental hospitals. The judges declared that knowledgeable consent to psychosurgery for altering violent behavior was "literally impossible" because of an almost universal lack of knowledge on the subject. The judges further stated in their unanimous decision that voluntary consent was not possible because the patient was in an "inherently coercive atmosphere even though no direct pressures may be placed on him." According to the judges, "Involuntarily confined patients cannot reason as equals with the doctors and administrators over whether they should undergo psychosurgery." It is noteworthy that the judges observed that "government has no power or right to control minds, thoughts and expressions." This decision should be encouraging to those who are concerned about the possible abuse of psychosurgery and to those who feel that psychosurgery itself is an abuse. There are still a number of ethical issues which must be answered before we implant electrodes or perform psychosurgery to control behavior.

Oil the squeaky wheel

Ervin's idea of self-control of our brain waves to control violent behavior is a positive step. Another step towards reducing the level of violence is the reduction of the psychological and socio-economic instigators of violence together with the creation of more effective institutions for its control. This might be accomplished by raising children in an environment which gives or withholds praise rather than giving corporal punishment. Behavior modification processes give many examples of the ability to change behavior by the giving of praise or a reward when a child does something good or the withholding of praise or a reward when he does something contrary to the accepted code of behavior. The unacceptable conduct is ignored and the good conduct is rewarded. As a result the child usually modifies his behavior to receive praise or rewards.[29]

At the present time the child whose behavior is antisocial receives the attention which he seeks from those around him. When he acts up he is scolded or punished in some way, but the child is at least getting someone to pay attention to him. The more the child acts up the more people pay attention to him. We actually seem to reinforce the negative behavior of the child. If the child knew that he had to behave himself to get the attention he desired, we might find children who spent as much time and effort at being "good" as they currently do at being "bad."

The school system could provide some help in this process of behavior modification by emphasizing in its curriculum those who were nonviolent. Should not Martin Luther King and Gandhi and others be glorified for their nonviolent struggle for social justice at least as much, if not more, than those who have violently fought for the same ideal. The schools must also provide all children the opportunity to obtain skills which will allow them to attain social and material rewards.

Aggression and violence may have a disastrous effect on the learning capacities of deprived children. In a study by Gardner,[30] it was found that an appreciable number of such children experience traumatic incidents and violent events during the first six years of their life. These children utilize a number of defenses against their fears and these defenses become the elements of neurotically-determined learning disabilities. Whatever type of defense the children choose will determine the type of learning disability they will manifest.

A very great step in reducing some violent behavior would be the removal of legitimate frustrations which a large number of people of all races suffer from in the world today. This can be done by providing good health care to all, by providing an opportunity for all to be educated in the schools of their choosing, by providing equal and real job opportunities for all people, by providing all people with the opportunity to involve themselves in the political processes and not just limiting political office to the few who can afford the cost of running for elective office. We must, in short, open up as many opportunities as possible for all people.

If we can alleviate the environmental problems which lead to violence we can certainly develop Dr. Ervin's idea of training people to control their brainwaves to prevent violence. This would certainly be a better solution to the problem of violence than psychosurgery or drugs. The individual would be in control of his own behavior and would not be manipulated by outside forces.

It boggles the mind to think of a nonviolent world, a world where love replaces violence. We have the potential to accomplish this. All we need is the desire.

---

[1]*Uniform Crime Reports for the United States* — 1962-1972 (yearly) (Washington, D.C.: United States Government Printing Office, 1963-1973).

[2]*Violent Crime: The Report of the National Commission on the Causes and Prevention of Violence.* (New York: George Braziller Co., 1969). p. 37.

[3]*Ibid.*, p. 42.

[4]*Ibid.*, p. 48.

[5]Frederic Wertham, *A Sign for Cain.* (New York: The Macmillan Co., 1966). pp. 35-42.

[6]Renatus Hartogs and Eric Artzt, *Violence: Causes and Solutions.* (New York: Dell Publishing Co.). pp. 15-20.

[7]Ashley Montagu, "Chromosomes and Crime," *Psychology Today*, 2: 43-49, October, 1968.

[8]*Ibid.*, p. 48.

[9]A. Bandura, D. Ross, and S.A. Ross, "Imitation of Film — Mediated Aggressive Models," *Journal of Abnormal and Social Psychology*, 66: 3-11, 1963.

[10]Hannah Arendt, *On Violence*. (New York: Harcourt, Brace and World, 1970). p. 65.

[11]Jerome D. Frank, "The Psychology of Violence," in *Violence The Crisis of American Confidence* ed. by Hugh Graham. (Baltimore: The Johns Hopkins Press, 1971). pp. 94-95.

[12]*Violent Crime: The Report of the National Commission on the Causes and Prevention of Violence* op. cit.

[13]Jerome D. Frank, *Op. cit.*, pp. 96-97.

[14]Konrad Lorenz, *On Aggression*, translated by Marjorie K. Wilson. (New York: Bantam Books, 1963) p. IX.

[15]Robert Ardrey, *African Genesis* (New York: Dell Publishing Co., 1961).

[16]Marvin E. Wolfgang, *Youth and Violence* (Washington, D.C.: U.S. Dept. of Health, Education and Welfare, 1970) p. 24.

[17]K. E. Moyer, "The Physiology of Violence," *Psychology Today*, 7: 35-38, July, 1973.

[18]Vernon H. Mark and Frank R. Ervin, *Violence and the Brain*. (New York: Harper and Row, 1970).

[19]K. E. Moyer, *op. cit.*, p. 35.

[20]J. H. Morton, H. Additon, R. G. Addison, et al. "A Clinical Study of Premenstrual Tension," *American Journal of Obstetrics and Gynecology*, 65: 1182-1191, 1953.

[21]José M. R. Delgado, "Cerebral Heterostimulation in a Monkey Colony," *Science*, 141: 161-163, 1963.

[22]M. Vergnes and P. Karli, "Elicitation of Mouse-killing Behavior by Electrical Stimulation of Medial Hypothalamus in the Rat," *Physiological Behavior*, 5: 1427-1430, 1970.

[23]K. E. Moyer, "The Physiology of Aggression and the Implications for Aggression Control" in *The Control of Aggression and Violence* ed. by Jerome L. Singer. (New York: Academic Press, 1971). p. 76.

[24]*Ibid.*, pp. 78-79.

[25]Vernon H. Mark and Frank R. Ervin, *op. cit.* also Harold M. Schmeck Jr., "Depths of Brain Probed for Sources of Violence," *The New York Times*, December 27, 1970, p. 1+.

[26]Donald Kenefick and Daniel Glaser, *The Violent Offender.* (New York: National Council on Crime and Delinquency, 1965).

[27]Richard A. Knox, "Violence: as Likely from Faulty Brain as Faulty Upbringing," *Boston Sunday Globe*, November 29, 1970, p. 4-A.

[28]Jean Dietz, "Boston's Psychosurgery: Success and Controversy," *Boston Sunday Globe*, January 21, 1973, p. 1-A.

[29]Albert Bandura, *Principles of Behavior Modification.* (New York: Holt, Rinehart and Winston, Inc., 1969). and Donald L. MacMillan, *Behavior Modification in Education.* (New York: The Macmillan Company, 1973).

[30]George E. Gardner "Aggression and Violence: The Enemies of Precision Learning in Children," *American Journal of Psychiatry,* 128: 445-450, October, 1971.

Other sources which the reader might find interesting are:

Lynne B. Iglitzin, *Violent Conflict in American Society.* (San Francisco: Chandler Publishing Co., 1972).

Roger N. Johnson, *Aggression in Man and Animals.* (Philadelphia: W.B. Saunders Co., 1972).

J. Krishnamurti, *Beyond Violence.* (New York: Harper and Row, 1973).

Rollo May, *Power and Innocence.* (New York: W.W. Norton & Co., Inc., 1972).

Larry Ng (editor), *Alternatives to Violence.* (New York: Time-Life Books, 1968).

Hans Toch, *Violent Men.* (Chicago: Aldine Publishing Co., 1969).

Chapter 6

❦❦❦ ❦❦❦ ❦❦❦ ❦❦❦ ❦ ❦❦❦❦❦

Chemicals Which Shape the Mind

This week, as you are reading this book, millions of your fellow Americans are taking chemicals of one type or another to control some aspect of their behavior. You, the reader, might be one of these millions who take some kind of sleeping pill or pep pill, or some form of tranquilizer or antidepressant, all prescribed by doctors. You may also be a member of a large group who take drugs; drugs not prescribed by a doctor and declared illegal by various statutes. Whatever the case, people have come to rely on chemicals to assist them without really being aware of the effects of chemicals on the brain. Because drugs do have some effect on behavior it seems certain that drugs must affect the chemistry of the brain in such a way that behavior can change. There are a number of chemicals present in the brain and research has shown that deficiencies of certain chemicals cause dysfunction in the brain. Studies have shown the need for proper nutrition in order for the child's brain to develop properly. In a study of 20 protein-calorie deficient children, ranging in age from one year to three-and-one-half years of age, a control group of 19 children without a history of malnutrition scored significantly higher than the malnourished children on 10 different sorting tests.[1]

In many states it is required by law that new born babies be tested for phenylketonuria (PKU). PKU is nearly always accompanied by mental retardation. The disease which can easily be detected by a urine test, is caused by the inability to metabolize the amino acid phenylalanine properly. The treatment for an infant who has PKU is accomplished by placing him on a diet free of phenylalanine. This treatment must begin early in infancy before irreversible damage occurs. If PKU is not treated the children will be slow in learning to walk and will usually never learn to form words. This is further evidence of the need for proper chemical balance in the system for the brain to function as it should.

In another study it was found that severe malnutrition, when it occurs very early in the life of experimental animals, permanently impairs the development of their brain and subsequent learning and behavior. The study further points out that in developing countries and, perhaps, in populations of slums and ghettos of the world's cities, malnutrition and the infection which is apt to follow have a very significant effect on children's ability to learn — an effect which may be more significant for the child than variations in family education, economic status, and cultural practices.[2]

Studies have also shown that starvation with prolonged under-nutrition affects the mind and that deprivation of single nutrients, such as niacin, may cause abnormalities of the central nervous system with alterations in mentation behavior and convulsive seizures. It has also been suggested that the higher incidence of prematurity and reduced ability found in children born in the spring months of the year may result from restricted maternal dietary intakes early in gestation because of the effects of heat in the preceding summer months.[3]

Other research has been performed which studied the total brain weight, protein, ribonucleic acid (RNA), and deoxyribonucleic acid (DNA) content in children who died of severe malnutrition during their first year of life in Santiago, Chile. The brains of the children were found to be reduced in weight and in nucleic acid content, compared to the brains of children of a similar age who had died of some cause other than malnutrition. The data from this study indicates that severe early malnutrition retards cell division in the human brain.[4]

Protein, DNA, and RNA have an important role in the function of cells, specifically in the area of protein synthesis. RNA, which plays an important role as an intermediary in protein synthesis, has been mentioned as a substance which might also have an important role in the learning process.

TABLE 6–1
FOODS UNSUITABLE FOR THE CHILD WITH PKU*

Milk	Meat
Cheese	Corn
Eggs	Wheat

*Since any food which contains protein also contains phenylal-anine, the child with PKU is placed on a protein-free diet and receives his essential amino acids (except for phenylalanine) just as he would receive vitamins – in the form of drops.

TABLE 6–2
FOODS SUITABLE FOR THE CHILD WITH PKU*

Vegetables		Fruits	
Asparagus	Cucumber	Apple	Grapes
Beans	Lettuce	Apricots	Oranges
Beets	Onion	Banana	Peaches
Broccoli	Radishes	Berries	Pears
Cabbage	Spinach	Cantaloupe	Pineapple
Carrots	Squash	Cherries	Plum
Celery	Tomato	Dates	Tangerine
		Figs	Watermelon

*These foods are not completely free of phenylalanine but when taken in the proper amount are safe for the child with PKU.

TABLE 6–3
AMINO ACIDS ESSENTIAL FOR
NORMAL GROWTH AND DEVELOPMENT

Threonine
Leucine
Isoleucine
Valine
Lysine
Methionine
Phenylalanine
Tryptophan

The following amino acids — Glycine, Alanine, Aspartic Acid, Glutamic Acid, Proline, Cystine, Hydroxyproline, Tyrosine, Serine, Arginine, and Histidine — can be manufactured by the body and are not as necessary for normal growth during adulthood as the above amino acids.

In an experiment reported by Faiszt and Gyorgy,[5] rats were taught to jump up on a shelf by conditioning them by pairing an acoustic stimulus with an electric shock. The rats which had been conditioned this way were then killed and their ground up brains were fed to other rats. These new rats demonstrated the same behavior. The substance responsible for the successful facilitation of learning came from the ribosomal RNA fraction from the rat brain.

In another experiment of the same nature, extracts rich in RNA were prepared from the brains of goldfish that had acquired and then extinguished a light-signaled avoidance to shock in an aquatic shuttle-box. Recipient fish which were injected intracranially with these extracts were able to extinguish the response significantly faster than other fish injected with extracts prepared from the brains of untrained fish.[6]

In another experiment, Vreeman[7] studied the specificity of information in intracranially injected RNA in a transfer experiment with 48 goldfish pretrained by equal stimuli in shock avoidance.

The injection of protein with molecular weights of more than 5000 led to considerably improved learning ability, while an injection of puromycin 24 hours before training lowered protein synthesis and yielded a significant decrease in learning ability. The results seem to indicate that protein is the raw material of the nerve cells and that the quantity of protein is proportional to the quality and stability of learning.

In earlier experiments of the same type in 1966 Agranoff[8] discovered that there were two types of memory: short term and long term. It was also found that there was a connection between the consolidation of memory and the manufacture of protein in the brain in Agranoff's experiments. Another important conclusion based on subsequent studies by Agranoff was the idea that memory fixation was blocked when the organism was in an environment associated with a high level of stimulation. To Agranoff this seemed to indicate that the formation of memory is environment-dependent and the consolidation of memory is time-dependent. Based on these studies Agranoff believes that learning and memory can be viewed as a form of biological development.

Dr. Holger Hyden of the University of Göteborg in Sweden has found that the amount of RNA in the brain increases as animals mature and acquire new experiences. The more experiences the animal has, the more information it acquires from its surroundings. This, in turn, causes more RNA to be produced by the brain cells.

In an attempt to find out more about the relationship between RNA and memory, Hyden analyzed the chemical content of brain cells from rats, rabbits, and other animals trained in his laboratory before and after learning had occurred. Hyden found, as a result of his experiments, that any kind of training or experience increased the level of RNA in the animal's brain cells. He also found that the type of RNA produced depended on the kind of experience. When a rat was trained to climb a wire, the RNA in Deiter's neuron cells increased and its base composition changed. Similar results were obtained in the cortical neuron cells when the dexterity of the left and right side of a rat was transferred. These findings suggest that different kinds of RNA are produced in the brain by different kinds of experiences.[9]

Similar experiments at other laboratories produced the same results. Dr. Hyden believes, since it is the job of RNA in the cell to control the production of other protein molecules, that memories may be "printed" into these new molecules. This would allow numerous copies of a memory to be produced and distributed throughout the brain and it would explain why memory cannot be destroyed by the removal of a section of the brain. RNA appears to be, at the least, an important link in the chain of electro-chemical events that produces our memory of the past.[10]

Dr. Georges Ungar of Baylor College of Medicine in Houston has isolated and identified the first component of what may be a system of molecular coding by which information is processed in the brain.

Research in the area of memory transfer involves inducing learned behavior in an animal. After the behavior has been learned, the animal is killed and the brain is removed and processed in such a way as to provide a substance that can be injected into the brain of an untrained animal. Many of the untrained animals demonstrate the same behavior as that which had been learned by the donor animal.

Dr. Ungar trained 4000 rats to acquire a fear of the dark. The training was accomplished by giving rats an electric shock whenever they chose a dark enclosure rather than a lighted one. From these 4000 donor rats, Dr. Unger obtained 5 kilograms of brain from which a substance, scotophobin, was isolated. Injection of a minute quantity of scotophobin into mice changed their normal preference for the dark into a fear of the dark.

In a similar experiment, Dr. Ungar used an electric shock to train fish to avoid one side or the other of their tanks which had been painted different colors. The color preference was passed on to other fish which received the ground up brain extract from the original learners.

If these substances can be synthesized, then it is possible that we can learn what specific chemical or combination of chemicals is produced in a particular learning situation and synthesize it so that it may be given to others who wish to learn a particular task.

This could have tremendous implications for improving the brain functions of the mentally retarded and the senile. It may also be possible, according to Ungar, to use this process to cure alcoholics and drug addicts. This could be done by isolating the chemicals that will make a rat fear alcohol or a particular drug. Once this is determined, experiments will need to be conducted to determine if these methods are applicable to humans.[11]

The late Dr. D. Ewen Cameron of the Veterans Administration Hospital in Albany, New York gave a drug, magnesium pemoline, to patients suffering severe memory losses. Some of the patients recovered to such a degree that they were able to leave the hospital and return to work. The drug, which seemed to assist in the production of RNA in the brain, was also effective in helping to improve the memory of elderly patients suffering from senility.

Ribaminol is a drug which affects the production of brain protein and has been found to be capable of producing a twofold increase in learning ability. Another drug, metrazol, stimulates the central nervous system and helps convert short-term memory into long-term memory.

Dr. James L. McGaugh of the University of California at Riverside has tested metrazol on two groups of mice with different hereditary backgrounds. When the mice were given a certain amount of metrazol they showed a forty per cent improvement in learning ability over mice that did not receive the drug.[12]

Since memory and the learning process can be facilitated or eliminated chemically and since learning of a very basic nature can be transferred from one animal to another chemically it seems that we should attempt to identify the specific chemicals which produce learning of a particular nature. If we could identify and then synthesize these chemicals, we could produce learning merely by injecting the substance into an individual.

It would certainly shake up our educational system if all that a person had to do to learn Calculus or Chemistry or English was to be injected with a specific chemical. Yet, this is very much within the realm of possibility. And, as mentioned earlier, it would also be possible to use these specific chemicals to cure drug or alcohol addiction.

Dr. Sidney Cohen of the UCLA Medical school has stated that, in functional terms, human intelligence or learning ability seems to depend on three different skills. The first skill involves the ability of an individual to pay attention or to concentrate. The next skill involves the brain being able to lay down some sort of lasting memory trace in the form of changed RNA molecules or in the form of proteins manufactured under the direction of RNA or in chemical changes at the synapses. Finally, one must have a retrieval system, a method of scanning memory traces and focusing on the right one. According to Dr. Cohen, all three processes could possibly be improved chemically. There appears to be no reason why chemicals could not be developed that would improve our thinking abilities.

There are any number of studies which point to the possible role of RNA in the learning process.[13]

There are also other chemicals which have been demonstrated to improve the learning process and short term memory. Centrophenoxine is such a substance which has significantly improved the learning process and short term memory for chronic alchoholics to whom it was given.

Alchohol has been found to be a substance which considerably decreases protein synthesis in the brains of mice. Since the bio-chemistry of the brain of mice and men is similar it would seem that alcohol could also reduce protein synthesis in the brain of man. This seems to be substantiated by the fact that many alcoholics suffer from disburbances of memory, orientation, judgement and comprehension. It is possible that long-term use of alcohol by man can cause sufficient damage to the brain to permanently impair these functions. Recent studies have shown the major importance of protein synthesis in memory function, learning, and behavior.

CHEMICALS WHICH SHAPE THE MIND

We have probably at one time or another heard of deficiency diseases caused by the lack of particular vitamins in the diet. Scurvy is an example of such a deficiency disease caused by the lack of vitamin C in a person's diet. In much the same way, deficiencies in the diet have an adverse effect on the brain and mental functioning. For the brain to function properly there must be an adequate supply of protein, iodine, vitamin A, thiamine, riboflavin and vitamin B_{12}.[14]

Dr. Linus Pauling believes that the mentally ill person does not get enough of these substances, or, if he does, he burns them off faster or cannot produce them as efficiently as needed. According to Pauling, the way to treat such an individual is to determine the deficiency and then correct it. This process is called orthomolecular psychiatry which means to provide the right amount of the right molecules at the right time and at the right place.

Studies have been done which indicate that an electrolyte imbalance may cause dementia and depression. In both dementia and depression there is a loss of potassium and a retention of sodium. In the depressed person, there is a loss of potassium from the cell with a corresponding entry of sodium. In demented people, there is an actual loss of cells together with some potassium loss from living cells which may be the initial stage in the breakdown of the cell.

Biochemical research on mental illness has shown that many of these illnesses may be caused by purely chemical deficiencies in the brain or body or by an imbalance of enzyme systems, a knowledge of which could lead directly to successful remedies.

A number of drugs have appeared on the market in the past few years to relieve depression. Electroshock therapy (EST) has also been used with success to treat depression. Senator Thomas Eagleton of Missouri, the original choice of Senator George McGovern as his running mate in the 1972 presidential campaign, is probably the best-known person to undergo electroshock therapy. Usually a combination of drugs, possibly electroshock therapy and psychotherapy are used in the treatment of depression. As further evidence is found linking depression with chemical abnormalities in the brain, it is likely that more effective drugs will be discovered to treat it.

Various drugs have been found to produce different states of mind in the people taking them. Reserpine, a drug used in the treatment of high blood pressure, has caused depressive symptoms in a number of patients. Another drug, iproniazid, developed for the treatment of tuberculosis, produces a feeling of euphoria in the patient. Studies with animals suggest that both of these drugs have an effect on two of the chemicals which help carry nerve impulses from one cell to another. It is believed that reserpine depletes the amount of serotonin and norepinephrine to make the patient depressed. Iproniazid produces an opposite effect by increasing the level of norepinephrine in the patient.

Studies are currently being conducted to further determine what part these chemicals play in producing depression. In one study it was found that the brains of suicide victims contained lower amounts of a serotonin byproduct than did the brains of normal people killed in accidents. It has also been found that the level of the norepinephrine byproduct is lower in the urine in some depressive patients than in the urine of normal individuals.

There are a number of drugs on the market to cure depression. One group of anti-depressants is related to iproniazid and functions by blocking the action of an enzyme in the brain that breaks down norepinephrine. This maintains the level of norepinephrine to prevent depression. Another group of drugs, called tricyclics, prevent the breakdown of serotonin.

While these drugs are beneficial to those suffering from depression they can have some very harmful side effects if not taken under a physician's direction. Some of the drugs which block the action of the enzyme that breaks down norepinephrine cause a sharp rise in blood pressure if taken with such foods as chocolate or cheese. The other drugs, the tricyclics can cause drowsiness, tremors, and muscular rigidity similar to the symptoms of Parkinson's disease.

Dr. Kenneth Clark has proposed the development of psycho-technology, the development of new drugs that could routinely be given to people, especially leaders holding great power, to subdue hostility and aggression and, thereby, allow more humane and intelligent behavior to emerge. This idea was set forth by Dr. Clark in September, 1971 at the annual convention of the American Psychological Association. In his speech Dr. Clark said that recent studies of electrical and chemical control of the brain "suggest that we might be on the threshold of that type of scientific biochemical intervention which could stabilize and make dominant the moral and ethical propensities of man and subordinate, if not eliminate, his negative and primitive behavioral tendencies."

Dr. Clark, a psychology professor at City College of New York, feels that the first priority in psychotechnology is the development of a medication that would be taken by national leaders to reduce their propensities to respond to an international crisis by initiating a nuclear war. The second priority would be the use of similar drugs on a much wider scale, according to Clark. This would include a type of chemical regulator as a condition of elective or military office. Another type of chemical regulator would be the standard dosage for all other individuals.

Dr. Clark has stated that he realizes the possible dangers of psychotechnology and that it is not his intention to create a race of human robots. It is his hope that psychotechnology can be used to enhance positive aspects such as empathy and kindness and to reduce the cruel and barbaric in man while maintaining the creative, evaluative, and selective capacities of man.

What Dr. Clark proposed in 1971 will be possible of accomplishment within the next few years. We have already seen the effects of electrical stimulation of the brain and so far in this chapter we have seen that certain drugs have a particular effect on our emotions, our memory, and our learning processes.

The more one reads about research under way, the more likely it seems that a pill, such as Dr. Clark mentioned, could be produced. We already have pills that eliminate depression, tranquilize us, produce euphoria, and heighten sensory awareness. Those who are opposed to Dr. Clark's view respond that although it may be possible to reduce human aggression through a pill it is not possible to eliminate a person's feelings that in some cases he should respond aggressively. His opponents feel that if unjust social systems and dehumanizing institutions are eliminated there will be no need for such a pill. In the meantime researchers continue in their attempt to develop the type of pill Dr. Clark proposed.

In chapter three the possibilities of electrical stimulation of the brain were explored. There is still another type of stimulation known as chemical stimulation of the brain (CSB). In CSB fine tubes are inserted in the brain and various chemicals can be introduced to the brain through the tubes to produce changes in emotion. A number of different chemicals can be administered to the brains of animals by a relatively simple procedure. Tiny hollow guide shafts are implanted in the animals' brains in order to deliver chemicals to selected areas of the brain. By means of a three-dimensional brain map and a stereotactic machine, which holds the head of the anesthetized animal and guides the surgical instruments, the location of each guide shaft is carefully established. After a tiny hole has been made in the skull and brain, a guide shaft is inserted and antiseptically fastened to the skull with jewelers' screws and adhesive. The number of shafts which can be inserted varies from one type of animal to the next. In a rat four or five shafts may be inserted while as many as 100 may be inserted in a monkey. Through these shafts it is possible to deliver as little as one microgram of a chemical in crystalline form or as little as a ten-thousandth of a milliliter of a solution.[15]

An early attempt at chemical stimulation of the brain occurred in 1954 when Dr. Alan Fisher injected the male sex hormone, testosterone, into specific sites in the hypothalamus of male rats. Dr. Fisher expected that this injection would stimulate male sex behavior. The behavior that occurred, however, was completely unexpected. The rat, after being injected in the brain with testosterone, became very restless. When the female rat was placed in the cage the male rat did not make sexual advances as it was expected he would. Instead he grasped the female by the tail with his teeth and dragged her across the cage to a corner. When he let go of her she ran away but he picked her up and brought her back again. This process was repeated several times. Dr. Fisher finally surmised that the male rat was displaying some form of maternal behavior. To test this idea he placed some newborn baby rats and strips of paper in the middle of the cage. The male took the paper and proceeded to build a nest in a corner of the cage. When the nest was completed the baby rats were placed in it by the male. The effect of the chemical injection lasted about thirty minutes but was renewed with another injection. A number of similar experiments led to the conclusion that a particular type of behavior was attributable to a specific chemical implanted at a specific site in the brain.

It has been found that there are several regions in the brain which help to control the hunger and thirst drives. Some of the regions that help to control the eating and hunger drive are located in the hypothalamus.

Sebastian B. Grossman, while still a Yale University graduate student, found that eating and drinking could be elicited in rats by brain injections of noradrenaline and acetylcholine, long known as transmitters of nerve impulses. When noradrenaline was injected into a site in the brain of a rat just above the hypothalamus the rat would begin to eat even if it had just been fed. When acetylcholine was injected into the identical area the rat would begin to drink even if it had just finished drinking before the injection. Chemicals that have been used to block the transmitting action of noradrenalin and acetylcholine at nerve synapses have been found also to be able to block the stimulating effects on the brain.

From Grossman's experiment it can be seen that different chemicals, even though injected at exactly the same site in the brain, release different inherent drives. Because of this, Dr. Fisher felt that the neurons composing each of the major drive circuits were chemically selective and would respond only to an appropriate chemical stimulus. According to Dr. Fisher's theory, a specific chemical could be released in the midst of several quite separate circuits but would selectively excite only one of them. This would make it possible to probe various parts of the brain with a specific chemical and actually chart the circuit responsive to the particular stimulus.

Dr. Fisher has charted the circuit that mediates drinking and has found that it has certain parallels to D.O. Hebb's model of the memory system in the brain. It is Hebb's belief that simple perceptual learning involves hundreds of neurons dispersed throughout the brain and that it is established gradually by the development of neuronal interconnections. The pattern of sensory, associational, and motor neurons is at first a simple one which may or may not last. As the perception is repeated and the neurons involved work together as a team, their functional interconnections become more firmly established. As the perception continues to be repeated, alternate pathways develop and the system becomes less vulnerable to disruption. This model of Hebb's helps to explain why it is that long-established memories are less apt to be lost through stress or brain damage than are memories of recent events.

The thirst-drive system is also solidly established with a number of alternative pathways. It differs from the memory system though in that most of its neuronal interconnections are present at birth since they were established by genetic inheritance.

There are a number of substances which are classified as legal drugs — caffeine, nicotine, and alcohol which affect the mind. People who use these substances habitually have developed an addiction for them, an addiction which may be just as serious as an addiction for an illegal drug.

Alcohol is a drug which causes a number of things to happen to its users. An alcoholic may suffer from a number of diseases which result from the toxic effects of alcohol, from the malnutrition associated with alcoholism, or from a combination of both. The central and peripheral nervous systems seem to be most susceptible to damage from the abuse of alcohol.

Alcohol exerts a depressant action on neurons in certain portions of the nervous system. If a person ingests enough alcohol so that the level of alcohol is 500 milligrams per 100 milliliters of blood, a deep coma will result. If the alcohol concentration is raised to 550 milligrams per 100 milliliters of blood the result is often fatal. At 250 to 300 milligrams of alcohol per 100 milliliters of blood an individual will show a weaving gait, loss of self-control, slurred speech, and lack of muscular coordination. The earliest changes, indicative of neurological impairment, appear in all persons at a blood level of 100 to 150 milligrams per 100 milliliters.

One of the problems faced by an alcoholic who uses alcohol as a food as well as a drug is that he is at the borderline of malnutrition of protein, the B complex vitamins, and minerals. This lack of nutrients certainly plays an important part as an explanation for the resultant brain damage suffered by alcoholics.

There are a number of other drugs which affect man in a variety of ways. LSD (lysergic acid diethylamide) is one such hallucinogenic drug which produces changes in the individual in four areas: perception, affect, cognition, and significance of perceptions.

The individual's perception, in particular his vision, is distorted. These distortions may take the form of illusions or hallucinations. To the person who has taken LSD, colors appear to be sharper, the walls and ceiling and floor may appear to move in and out, and two-dimensional pictures appear to be three-dimensional. Other senses also seem to be made more acute by LSD.

In the cognitive area there are some changes which occur in the individual under the influence of LSD. It sometimes becomes difficult for the individual using LSD to differentiate between past, present and future. Very often there is a distortion of body image or body pattern. Often the individual also experiences a feeling of being at one with the universe.

The fourth area of change is one in which the individual seems to experience feelings of insight, illumination, revelation, and expanded consciousness.[16]

At the present time the potential usefulness of LSD is being explored with three groups of people: alcoholics, neurotics, and dying patients. It appears that LSD therapy may have a place in the treatment of these conditions.

Other hallucinogenic drugs are mescaline, dimethyltryptamine, diethyltryptamine, and STP. The effects of these drugs are similar to those of LSD.

Marijuana is a drug which, although illegal in this country, is undergoing a process of "decriminalization," which is an attempt to make it legal, in several States. Studies indicate that use of marijuana does not result in physical or physic dependence or tolerance. Psychological dependence does occur to some degree in people using marijuana but the same type of psychological dependence is found in those who smoke and those who drink alcohol.

The effects of marijuana are similar to, but not as strong as LSD. Marijuna is used by many young people because of the pressure by the peer group to conform, and also because of the pleasures of taking it. It is often used like alcohol as a relaxant.

Another type of drug which affects the mind is the barbiturate. Barbiturates induce a state of intoxication which is associated with errors in judgment and accident-proneness. A person who is suffering from barbiturate intoxication will usually have the following symptoms: sluggishness, slowed and slurred speech, defective memory, and rapid emotional changes, as well as deteriorated self-care. The barbiturates are potentially dangerous drugs as evidenced by their frequent use in suicides and the physical and psychic dependence they produce in users.

Amphetamines are a type of drug which have been associated with seriously impaired performance and judgement and in some cases with aggressive acting-out. In recent years amphetamine prescriptions have accounted for between 6 to 10 per cent of all prescriptions for any drugs. At least one out of every five adults, according to a California research group, admits to long-term or habitual use of ampehtamines. In some cities there is significant amphetamine abuse as early as the fifth and sixth grades and in other surveys of students it has been found that between 15 and 25 per cent of all high school students in a number of diverse communities are regular amphetamine users.[17]

Although the Food and Drug Administration (FDA) has recognized only a few legitimate areas for amphetamine usage there are still many physicians who prescribe them routinely for any number of reasons. The acceptable areas, according to the FDA, are short term appetite reductions, narcolepsy, some types of Parkinsonism, and certain behavioral disorders in hyperkinetic children.

Another type of drug which affects the mind is heroin, a member of the opiate family. The opiates induce apathy, docility, and listlessness in their users and yet they are responsible for a good deal of violent behavior. This violent behavior is caused by the need of the drug addict to get the money to pay for his drugs, not by the addiction itself.

One of the treatments for heroin addiction is methadone maintenance. Methadone is a narcotic which does not provide a "high" for the addict as does heroin.One of the problems of the methadone maintenance program centers around this point. The heroin addict, while on heroin, experiences a pleasurable high. On methadone he does not experience this pleasurable high.

Syanon is another approach to the problems of the heroin addict. Syanon, which is similar in theory to Alcoholics Anonymous, is a self-help program for addicts. Complete abstinence from drugs, as well as the techniques of group support and encounter therapy, are used to help addicts overcome their habits. It has been suggested by Andrew Weil[18] that it would be more useful to show addicts how they can get highs in other ways even by getting them to go from one drug to another less harmful one rather than by asking them to abstain from drugs completely. Weil suggests that nitrous oxide, also known as laughing gas, might be useful for this purpose because it provides a type of experience that heroin users seem to like. An advantage to this program is that people who have experimented with nitrous oxide are more apt to be encouraged to try meditation as a means of altering consciousness than are heroin addicts.

Weil, who has done considerable research on drug addiction and drug addicts, believes that we are born with a drive to experience episodes of altered consciousness and that as children grow they discover chemical methods of altering their consciousness. The use of illegal drugs, according to Weil, is "nothing more than a logical continuation of a developmental sequence going back to early childhood." Weil believes in this developmental scheme because he has seen it in hundreds of drug users he has interviewed and known. He, like just about all of us, has also experienced it in the act of spinning around. If we think back to our childhood days we can remember whirling around until we collapsed dizzily on the ground with the world spinning around us. This was an altered state of consciousness which was a part of our development.

If this is true, and Weil presents convincing arguments for it, we must realize that it is natural for people to want to alter their consciousness. The problem of drug abuse then becomes a problem of finding a better alternative to altering a consciousness than drugs. According to Weil, drug dependence, whether the drug is alcohol, heroin or marijuana, is "essentially an error of thinking, not a pharmacological or biochemical phenomenon, even though it may be accompanied by changes in the physical body."

Weil believes that the use of drugs does not hurt the body or the mind in the way that most physicians or psychiatrists think. The greatest harm from drugs lies in their keeping people from reaching "the goal of consciousness developed to its highest potential." Drug-users have given up drugs for meditation. Meditation may possibly be an answer to the problem of altering consciousness in a way that provides a better high than the highs obtained through drugs. One benefit of meditation as opposed to drugs is that one does not develop a tolerance for meditation. The drug user, on the other hand, depends on drugs to alter his consciousness and gradually builds up such a tolerance to drugs that he can no longer get high on his usual dosage. When this happens he must either increase the dosage or turn to a stronger drug. In either of these cases he is no longer in control of the situation. He cannot alter his consciousness by himself but must depend on some outside agent to do it for him.

A reasonable approach to the problem of drug abuse would seem to be one which would allow people to experience the high of altering their own state of consciousness through such techniques as meditation or biofeedback. Perhaps the solution to the drug problem is as simple as teaching young children to meditate and control their bodily processes through a technique such as biofeedback.

Certain chemicals are needed for the brain to function properly. Without them the brain becomes dysfunctional. The idea is to maintain a proper balance of these necessary chemicals in the system. For those chemicals which produce harm to the system, such as drugs, the approach should be one of providing an alternative method of getting high without dependence on the drugs. As mentioned before, meditation and biofeedback provide two ways of accomplishing this.

---

[1]Lois M. Brockman and Henry N. Ricciuti, "Severe Protein-calorie Malnutrition and Cognitive Development in Infancy and Early Childhood," *Developmental Psychology.* 4 (3): 312-319, 1971.

[2]Nevin S. Scrimshaw, "Early Malnutrition and Central Nervous System Function," *Merrill-Palmer Quarterly.* 15:375-387, October, 1969.

[3]David Baird Coursin "Nutrition and Brain Function," in *Modern Nutrition in Health and Disease* 4th edition edited by Michael G. Wohl and Robert S. Goodhart. (Philadelphia: Lea and Febiger Publishing Co., 1968) pp. 1070-1085.

[4]Myron Winick and Pedro Rosso, "The effect of Severe Early Malnutrition on Cellular Growth of Human Brain," *Pediatric Research.* 3 (2): 181-184, 1969.

[5]Jozsef Faiszt and Adam Gyorgy, "Role of Different RNA Fractions from the Brain in Transfer Effect," *Nature.* 220: 367-368, October 26, 1968.

[6]William G. Braud, "Extinction in Goldfish: Facilitation by Intracranial Injection of RNA from Brains of Extinguished Donors," *Science.* 168 (3936): 1234-1236, 1970.

[7]Wolfgang Vreeman, "The Significance of RNA and Proteins for the Learning Process and Memory," *Studia Psychologia.* 13 (2) 102-113, 1971.

[8]Bernard W. Agranoff, "Memory and Protein Synthesis," *Scientific American.* 216 (6): 115-122, June, 1967.

[9]Takeo Deguchi, "On the Biochemical Theory of Learning," *Japanese Psychological Review.* 12:18-29, May, 1969.

[10]Russell Freedman and James E. Morriss, *The Brains of Animals and Man.* (New York: Holiday House, 1972) pp. 119-122.

[11]"Small Peptide Induces Fear of Darkness in Rats," *Chemical and Engineering News.* 49 (2): 27-28, January 11, 1971.

[12]Russell Freedman and James Morriss, *Op. cit.* pp. 132-135.

[13]These studies include:

Selby H. Evans, "Chemical Programming in the Brain: Speculations," *Journal of Biological Psychology.* 10 (1) 10-14, 1968.

Edward Glassman, "The Biochemistry of Learning: an Evaluation of the Role of RNA and Protein," *Annual Review of Biochemistry,* 38: 605-646, 1969.

Yechiel Becker, "A Theory on RNA Species in Nerve Cells and Their role in Brain Function and Drug Action," *Perspectives in Biology and Medicine.* 14 (4): 659-670, Summer, 1971.

[14]"Mental Disease: Biochemical Causes," *Nature.* 223 (5210): 999, September, 1969.

[15]Alan E. Fisher, "Chemical Stimulation of the Brain," *Scientific American* 210 (10): 60-68, June, 1964.

[16]Jerome Levine, "LSD — A Clinical Overview," *Drugs and the Brain* edited by Perry Black, (Baltimore: The Johns Hopkins Press, 1969) pp. 301-308.

[17]Lester Grinspoon and Peter Hedblom, "Amphetamines Reconsidered," *Saturday Review.* LV (28): 33-46 July 8, 1972.

[18]Andrew Weil, *The Natural Mind.* (Boston: Houghton Mifflin Company, 1972) pp. 71-72.

For additional information the reader might refer to:
Samuel Bogoch, *The Biochemistry of Memory*, (New York: Oxford University Press, 1968).

THE FUTURE: HUMAN ECOLOGY AND EDUCATION

Robert E. Bowman and Surinder P. Datta (Editors), *Biochemistry of Brain and Behavior.* (New York: Plenum Press, 1970).

Jack R. Cooper, Floyd E. Bloom, Robert H. Roth, *The Bio-chemical Basis of Neuropharmacology.* (New York: Oxford University Press, 1970).

William C. Corning and Martin Balaban, *The Mind, Biological Approaches to Its Functions.* (New York: Interscience Publishers, 1968).

Helen H. Gifft, Marjorie B. Washbon, Gail G. Harrison, *Nutrition, Behavior and Change.* (Englewood Cliffs: Prentice-Hall, 1972).

Judith Groch, *You and Your Brain.* (New York: Harper and Row, 1963).

A. R. Luria, *Human Brain and Psychological Processes.* translated by Basil Haigh (New York: Harper and Row, 1966).

Arnold J. Mandell and Mary P. Mandell, (editors) *Psychochemical Research in Man.* (New York: Academic Press, 1969).

Clifford T. Morgan, *Physiological Psychology,* 3rd edition. (New York: McGraw-Hill, 1965).

John Nash, *Developmental Psychobiology.* (Englewood Cliffs: Prentice-Hall, 1970).

V.D. Nebylitsyn and J.A. Gray, *Biological Bases of Individual Behavior.* (New York: Academic Press, 1972).

Psychobiology. (San Francisco: W.H. Freeman & Co., 1966).

J. H. Quastel and David M. J. Quastel, *The Chemistry of Brain Metabolism in Health and Disease.* (Springfield, Ill.: Charles C. Thomas, Publisher, 1961).

John Taylor, *The Shape of Minds to Come.* (New York: Weybright and Talley, 1971.

Otto Walaas (editor) *Molecular Basis of Some Aspects of Mental Activity.* Vol. 1 and Vol. 2 (New York: Academic Press, 1966 and 1967).

Nigel Calder, *The Mind of Man.* (New York: The Viking Press 1970)

Gordon Claridge, *Drugs and Human Behavior.* (Baltimore: Penguin Books, Inc., 1970.

CHEMICALS WHICH SHAPE THE MIND

Robert M. Featherstone and Alexander Simon (editors), *A Pharmacologic Approach to the Study of the Mind*. (Springfield, Ill.: Charles C. Thomas, Publishers, 1959).

Charles T. Tart (editor), *Altered States of Consciousness*. (New York: John Wiley & Sons, 1969).

R. C. Zoehner, *Zen, Drugs and Mysticism*. (New York: Pantheon Books, 1972).

Chapter 7

✿✿✿ ✿✿ ✿✿✿✿✿✿ ✿✿✿ ✿✿✿ ✿✿✿ ✿✿

The Hyperkinetic Child

In March, 1971, a panel of child psychiatrists and drug experts, called together by the Department of Health, Education and Welfare, concluded that there were a million children suffering from hyperkinesis in the United States. With this many children affected by hyperkinesis it is necessary to take a closer look at who is hyperkinetic and what the hyperkinetic child is like.

When young, the hyperkinetic child breaks things or tears things apart because these activities are simple to perform. He is always moving about and this sometimes leads to mischievious behavior. He is constantly in trouble because of his restlessness, noisiness, and disobedience.

A study of hyperkinetic children, to describe the nature and incidence of their symptoms, was conducted by Mark Stewart[1] while he was associated with the Washington University School of Medicine in St. Louis. He selected a group of hyperkinetic children, and compared them with a control group of normal children. The hyperkinetic children, between the ages of 5 and 11, all showed symptoms of overactivity and inability to maintain concentration.

Most children at sometime or another display either individual characteristics or groups of these characteristics. Parents reading this need not be alarmed if they see some of these characteristics in their own children from time to time. It is when most of these

104

characteristics are found in children most of the time that one should consider whether the child is hyperkinetic or not.

In the study done by Stewart a number of mothers of hyperkinetic children began to notice that their child was different before he was two years old. Many of the children had a history of feeding problems, disturbed sleep, and generally poor health in the first year of life. Many had also been handicapped by delayed speech development and poor coordination. There was nothing to indicate that these problems were due to complications in the mother's pregnancy or delivery or to a family history of mental disorders, according to Stewart.

Dr. Maurice Laufer,[2] on the other hand, does feel that hyperkinesis can be a consequence of poor implantation of the ovum, threatened miscarriage, maternal illness, or medications during pregnancy. He also believes that it may be due to some abnormality of the birth process — being born with the cord around the neck, or from the pressures of being delivered even if the delivery is normal.

Stewart found that an unexpectedly large number of hyperkinetic children have had a history of accidental poisoning, usually before they reach the age of three. The hyperkinetic child, because he is always moving about and getting into things, is more apt to be exposed to poison from cleaning fluids or medicine cabinets than the child who is not hyperkinetic. The mother's warning not to touch is actually an incentive for the hyperkinetic child to touch and taste and otherwise explore. This would seem to indicate that hyperkinetic children are abnormal from birth; that hyperkinesis is not something they catch from someone or learn from someone, but is something they are born with.

Boys are more apt to be hyperkinetic than girls and this is not because of biased treatment of boys by teachers and parents. It seems to be inborn as are other difficulties such as delayed speech development and reading disabilities which are also more characteristic of boys than girls. Stewart has hypothesized that this could be due to some sex-linked inherited abnormality or to some weakness in the male nervous system.

The mothers of hyperkinetic children do not seem to be different from mothers of children who are not hyperkinetic. The fathers of hyperkinetic children, however, do differ very often from the fathers

THE FUTURE: HUMAN ECOLOGY AND EDUCATION

TABLE 7–1
COMMON SYMPTOMS OF HYPERACTIVE CHILDREN*

Overactive
Doesn't Finish Projects
Fidgets
Can't Sit Still at Meals
Doesn't Stay With Games
Wears Out Toys, Furniture, etc.
Talks Too Much
Doesn't Follow Directions
Clumsy
Fights With Other Children
Unpredictable
Teases
Doesn't Respond to Discipline
Gets Into Things
Speech Problems
Temper Tantrums
Doesn't Listen to Whole Story
Defiant
Hard to Get to Bed
Irritable
Reckless
Unpopular with Peers
Impatient
Lies
Accident Prone
Enuretic
Destructive

*Adapted from Mark A. Stewart, "Hyperactive Children", Scientific American April, 1970

106

of children who are not hyperkinetic. The fathers of hyperkinetic children have usually been troublesome when they were children themselves. A number of fathers of hyperkinetic children in the Stewart study were school dropouts and as adults were restless and short-tempered.

Hyperkinesis is not restricted to children. It is not something which a child automatically outgrows. Teen-agers who are hyperkinetic are still restless, unable to concentrate on a task or finish it, and are overtalkative and poor in school performance. Many have low self-esteem, and feel as if they are being picked on. They are more impatient and irritable than they were as children. A number of hyperkinetic teen-agers engage in various forms of deviant behavior. Many of them are not interested in school and are behavior problems in school.[3]

Many adults are also hyperkinetic and have a number of the same symptoms as hyperkinetic children and teen-agers do. As Stewart points out, some of these characteristics — high energy, aggressiveness, and lack of inhibitions — may actually be helpful to the adult in his work but they definitely handicap and produce problems for the child who is forced to sit still and study for a long period of time.

This finding by Stewart is in disagreement with that of Laufer who states that the hyperkinesis always disappears in time.[4] Dr. Gordon J. Millichap, Professor of Neurology and Pediatrics at Northwestern University Medical School and pediatric neurologist at Children's Memorial Hospital, Chicago, believes there no longer is a need for drug therapy with the hyperkinetic child once he reaches the age of 12 because "in most cases treated hyperkinetic patients generally improve as they grow older."[5]

Some hyperkinetic children face the problem of having accumulated such a large number of antisocial habits and having such a poor school preparation that they are not able to make it in our society. As a result, these people turn away from society and, especially if from a low socio-economic class, become delinquent.

A team of psychiatrists, who examined children referred to the hyperkinesis clinic of Gateways Hospital, Los Angeles, attempted to apply electroencephalography to the diagnosis and treatment of hyperkinesis. Their findings indicate that there may be a delayed central nervous system maturation in hyperkinetic children. In this study directed by Dr. James H. Satterfield, children, between the ages of six and nine, sat in easy chairs while viewing a videotaped cartoon. The children were subjected to brief but loud clicks. Analysis of the EEG's showed that the hyperkinetic children had "significantly lower evoked cortical response amplitudes and longer latencies than the age-matched controls."[6] This was interpreted by Dr. Satterfield and his colleagues to mean that the central nervous system matures later in hyperkinetic children than in normal children. The most common EEG abnormality noticed was an excessive amount of slow-wave activity which is consistent with delayed maturation of the central nervous system.

A good deal of research has been done in the area of treating hyperkinesis. Charles Bradley of the Emma Pendleton Bradley Home in Providence, Rhode Island, discovered many years ago that stimulating drugs, such as the amphetamines, calmed hyperactive children and improved their behavior. Sedatives, on the other hand, tended to increase the activity of a hyperkinetic child.

When a hyperkinetic child is given an amphetamine he usually becomes quiet, has a longer attention span, is easier to get along with, and generally performs better in school. Amphetamines have much the same effect on normal people who must perform boring tasks. It seems that the amphetamine causes the individual to focus all of his attention on a task.

The amphetamine acts on the reticular formation in the brain stem, an area controlling consciousness and attention. Amphetamines affect the metabolism of norepinephrine in the brain cells by stimulating its release from nerve endings. Norepinephrine, injected into a rat, lowers the rat's activity level and responsiveness. Injection of acetylcholine has an opposite effect. Perhaps the amphetamine acts on the hyperkinetic child to activate norepinephrine or to restore the balance between acetylcholine and norepinephrine.

Anxiety can also cause the release of norepinephrine in the brain cells. This could explain why hyperkinetic children behave so differently from what they usually do when they are placed in stress situations. The symptoms of hyperkinetic behavior are usually displayed only when the child feels at home.

Mary Coleman[7] in a study she conducted, has also shown the need for a chemical balance to reduce hyperkinesis. Where the serotonin concentration was low, the children being studied were hyperkinetic. When the serotonin concentration rose to a normal level, the children's hyperkinesis lessened. This would appear to strengthen the idea that hyperkinesis has a biological basis.

A California allergist, Dr. Ben F. Feingold, speaking at an American Medical Association symposium in New York in June, 1973, proposed the theory that artificial flavorings and colorings in almost every food were the cause of widespread hyperkinetic activity in children. The chemical additives, which Dr. Feingold blamed, were the salicylates which make up 80 percent of all food additives.

Dr. Feingold reported that he was able to turn off unruly behavior in fifteen severely hyperkinetic children by keeping them away from soda pop, ice cream, puddings, gelatin, hot dogs, most breakfast cereals, and snacks and convenience foods containing certain additives. Some of these children had been controlled before only by drugs. Ten other children failed to respond to the diet treatment.

There seems to be circumstantial evidence, even though there is no absolute scientific evidence, to support Dr. Feingold's theory. As evidence is being collected, Dr. Feingold is advocating a ban on salicylate-based colorings and flavorings, especially in foods likely to be consumed by children.

John Ott[8] has conducted an interesting study which would seem to point to the lighting environment in a classroom as a possible factor which might produce hyperactive behavior in children.

Ott's experiment involved four classes with a total of 100 first graders in windowless classes. Under these conditions some of the first graders being observed, demonstrated nervous fatigue, irritability, lapses of attention and hyperactive behavior. These students were active to an extreme degree. They were observed, by hidden cameras as they jumped out of their seats, flailed their arms and paid little or no attention to their teachers.

After three months of observations the lighting in two of the classrooms was changed from ordinary fluorescent lighting to full-spectrum, shielded lights which closely duplicate natural light. The ordinary flourescent lighting does not give off ultraviolet radiation which is found in sunlight. However, the full-spectrum shielded lights do.

Under the new lighting the students' behavior, as well as classroom performance, improved considerably. One student, who had been exceptionally active before the change in lighting, learned to read and was capable of independent study after the change in lighting.

In the other two cases, where the lighting remained unchanged, the students continued to exhibit hyperactive behavior.

As a result of this experiment, Philip Salvatore, Chairman of the Board of Obrig Industries in St. Petersburg, Florida, introduced full-spectrum, shielded lighting in his plant which manufactured contact lenses. The results, according to Salvatore, were a marked increase in labor output, a drop in absenteeism and a general improvement in morale.

More research is needed in this area but the results, so far, seem to indicate that lighting may be a possible cause of hyperactivity in children.

The use of amphetamines to treat hyperkinetics is successful with one-half to two-thirds of those on whom it is tried. Whatever way the amphetamines do their job may not be known with certainty, but what is known is that they do work and allow the central nervous system of the hyperkinetic child to function normally. They do their work through a kind of replacement chemotherapy that restores chemical balance to allow normal functioning of the central nervous system. Some amphetamines which are used to help restore this chemical balance in the hyperkinetic child are aventyl, benzedrine, dexedrine, Ritalin, and Tofranil. Since the cause of hyperkinesis is not known, it is only possible to treat it once it is noticed. This treatment, usually by amphetamines, is a cause of concern to many people.

Most people, unless they have had hyperkinetic children, have been unaware that there was such a condition as hyperkinesis and that its treatment involved the use of amphetamines. The Huntley-Brinkley news program of July 4, 1970 made people aware of the existence of such a problem. They were informed by Huntley and Brinkley that hundreds of school children in Omaha, Nebraska were being given so-called behavior modification drugs. These drugs were being administered to the children "to make them behave better in school." Controversy developed as a result of this report. The controversy revolved around the question of whether or not giving drugs to hyperkinetic children to improve their behavior in school was an infringement on their liberties.

There were also a number of other problems that disturbed people when they saw the Huntley and Brinkley program and read the ensuing reports of behavior modification in local newspapers. One of these problems involved the selection of school children who were to be given these drugs. How much trust should a physician place in a teacher's judgement? Teachers have classified as hyperkinetic, children who take their ballpoint pens apart or who just stop to talk with a classmate when they are returning from a pencil-sharpener.[9] If this type of evaluation of deviant behavior was acceptable to doctors who prescribe the drugs, people had a right to be very concerned. Fortunately, doctors did question many of the evaluations of teachers which labelled children as hyperkinetic. Another safeguard in this area was the fact that, if a child were incorrectly diagnosed as being hyperkinetic and had amphetamines prescribed for him he would usually become even more active. This would indicate to the doctor that it was possible that the diagnosis had been faulty.

Another problem with prescribing drugs for the hyperkinetic child is the possibility of addiction in the psychological sense. The child does not become addicted in the physical sense but does feel the need for the drug as a psychological crutch. Children taking amphetamines under medical supervision perceive the drugs as medicine which will eventually be given up.[10] It seems that the dangers of addiction are minimal for the hyperkinetic child receiving skilled medical treatment.

The problem of undesirable physiological side effects of the drugs being prescribed for the hyperkinetic child is another area of controversy. Doctors are aware of the possible side effects of the drugs which are being prescribed. As long as the drugs are used only as prescribed by the doctor, and with the consent of the parents, the possibility of bad side effects is reduced to a minimum.

Still another problem area occurs if the use of drugs prevents the hyperkinetic child from regulating his own behavior. This is a risk that is taken, but many people would say it is minor compared to the lack of freedom to regulate one's own behavior which occurs in most classrooms day in and day out. Control seems to be the obsession of teachers. As a result of this need to control, students have very little opportunity to develop self-discipline. They are told what to do, when to do it, and how to do it. This is exactly what people fear will happen to the hyperkinetic child who must take drugs — that he will lose his freedom of choice to govern his own behavior. In most schools this opportunity is not given anyway. The child who speaks out of turn, or who is noisy and disruptive, is a threat to the teacher and runs the risk of being tagged a "hyperkinetic."

In the state of Rhode Island, at the present time, there are approximately 6,000 school children between the ages of 5 and 13 who are taking drugs daily to control their hyperactivity. For a number, the results have been such that the child's behavior and progress in school have been aided greatly.

On the other hand, the story of David[11] shows the negative side of the drug controversy. David, at the age of thirteen, had been taking drugs to control his hyperactivity for a couple of years when he asked his mother to stop making him take his daily dosage of eight dexedrine tablets. He told his mother that his blood felt as if it "is curdling inside me and wants to burst out of my skin."

David's mother felt that she had been forced into drugging David. She tried to fight to keep her son from taking the drugs but was told by school officials that David might have to be expelled if he did not continue taking the drugs.

The pills took David's appetite away and he cried a good deal of the time. At night he would be unable to sleep and would walk the floor for hours at a time. When he was able to sleep, his dreams were so terrifying that he was unable to relate them to anyone.

It was so bad for David that one morning before school he collapsed and told his mother that he could not take his pills anymore. David's mother called the school to inform the officials that her son was not coming. As a result, Family Court action was initiated because of David's truancy. David was certainly not being helped by medication. It is very possible that David is one of the "90 per cent of the children in Rhode Island who are on these drugs and should not be on them," according to Dr. Paul Lamarche of the Rhode Island Hospital Child Development Clinic. Dr. Stanley Krippner of the Maimonides Children's Hospital in Brooklyn has stated that "a case could be made that some of the schools in Rhode Island have seized on hyperkinesis as a catch-all for their problem children, and on psychoactive drugs as a simplistic method of restraint.[12] Dr. Krippner holds the opinion that many school personnel are using medication as the first approach instead of as a last resort for children whose classroom behavior is divergent. Instead of using special education techniques to assist each overactive school child, an attempt is made to calm them by the easiest possible method — the use of medication.

The problem has also been noted by other doctors and psychiatrists who feel that many children, who are being referred to them as hyperkinetic, are simply restless or may have a learning problem. The danger in this area can readily be seen when children as young as twelve months old are undergoing drug therapy for, supposedly, hyperkinetic behavior. It can further be evidenced when children are sent home from school and their parents are told that the child will not be readmitted to school until he is put on some type of medication by a doctor.

It seems that many school administrators and teachers forget that the normal child has a good deal of energy which must be used up in some way. To place him in school and expect him to sit still for the school day is not realistic. Yet if he does not he could be labelled a hyperkinetic. He may not be hyperkinetic at all, but simply restless with the school environment, an environment in which he is all too often required to sit quietly with a minimal opportunity to use up any of his energy unless he uses it in a way which disrupts the "normal" routine of the classroom. If a child is disruptive, the question which is usually asked is "What's wrong with him?" We very seldom hear the question asked, "What is it about school that made him act that way?" or "What inappropriate demand did we make of him that caused him to act that way?" We do not seem to feel that it may be the school which is at fault and not the student. We overlook the ways in which the school contributes to the problem of restlessness in the child. A few hours of Physical Education per school week are not enough to allow the student to use up all the energy he has.

Dr. Eric Denhoff, a nationally known pediatric neurologist, believes that many of the children referred to him for drug therapy are really frustrated and need careful medical guidance and direction. He does not feel that medication alone is the answer. He feels that counseling and help in learning should be given along with medication. It is Dr. Denhoff's opinion that with counseling and learning help only about 10 percent of the children of a given age would need to be given medication to control their hyperactivity. Dr. Denhoff would like to see all preschool children examined for signs of hyperkinetic behavior before they entered kindergarten. He would also like to see hospitals keep records of all "risk" births to help in diagnosis of the hyperkinetic child. By doing these two things it would be possible to know better just who the ten percent of hyperkinetic children are who need drug therapy, according to Dr. Denhoff.

While there is a disagreement as to the extent of drug therapy needed to control hyperkinesis, the medical profession does agree that drug therapy is of value in a number of cases. There is also agreement that children should be extensively tested on an individual basis before drugs are prescribed and that drugs should not and cannot be substituted for a good educational program which allows the child to use his energy in a constructive way. Agreement also exists that drug therapy is not the solution to emotional stresses which develop within the family and cause a child to be disturbed or frustrated.

Medication, when used in addition to special educational programs and psychological guidance, can help make the hyperkinetic child more manageable in school. Additionally, this procedure can also help the hyperkinetic child to possibly achieve normal development over the long term.

Dr. Gerald Solomons, Director of the University of Iowa's Child Development Clinic and also Professor of Pediatrics at the University of Iowa College of Medicine, would like to see regional facilities set up to handle the large number of pupils referred by school systems as possible hyperkinetics. These centers would be staffed by experts in a number of disciplines. These experts would diagnose and prescribe treatment and see that adequate follow-up is maintained. The centers, according to Solomons, would be equipped to provide the entire family with counseling and other care because a poor home atmosphere can aggravate the behavioral problems of the hyperkinetic child.

Dr. Solomons believes that, until such centers are set up, the doctor must get information from sources outside the family as well as from the family itself before initiating drug therapy. He must also consider the parents' attitudes towards drugs and their ability to supervise their child's medication to insure that treatment is successful.

The parents and teachers of hyperkinetic children can help the child in a number of ways. All children need encouragement and praise, especially the hyperkinetic child. Teachers and parents should try to recognize and praise the child's positive traits rather than emphasizing the negative ones. If this is done, it may be possible to modify his undesirable habits one at a time.

The hyperkinetic child suffers when placed in a difficult environment or social system. He needs to know how to react and needs definite guidelines which he can follow. He should be protected from threatening situations and gradually introduced to new settings.

He should be aware of his own strengths and limitations and be able to make the best use of them. He should be given the opportunity to develop control over his own behavior by having his work periods broken up so that he does not become bored and hyperactive. He should play with only a few friends at a time for a short time. By doing these things he has a chance to develop control of his own behavior.

Most families with a hyperkinetic child need counseling help. They need help to learn how to react to the temper outbursts of the hyperkinetic child. The parents need help in teaching their child how to accept limits and how to delay gratification. The family needs help in setting up a structured, consistent, and calm atmosphere in which the hyperkinetic child can do well.[13] Perhaps the best way that all of this can be accomplished is through educating parents and teachers as to what problems a hyperkinetic child has and how the hyperkinetic child can be helped to overcome these problems. By realizing that the child has a problem and by being sympathetic and helpful we can help to provide the atmosphere which will allow the hyperkinetic child to function successfully in our society.

---

[1]Mark A. Stewart, "Hyperactive Children," *Scientific American.* 222: 94-98, April, 1970.

[2]Maurice W. Laufer, "Medications, Learning and Behavior," *Phi Delta Kappan*, 52: 169-170, November, 1970.

[3]Wallace Mendelson, Noel Johnson, Mark A. Stewart, "Hyperactive Children as Teenagers: A Follow-up Study," *Journal of Nervous Mental Diseases*, 153: 273-279, April, 1971.

[4]Laufer, *op. cit.*, p. 169.

[5]"Minimal Brain Dysfunction: A Consensus of Chemotherapy," *Hospital Practice*, July, 1972.

[6]*Ibid.*

[7]Mary Coleman, "Serotonin Concentrations in Whole Blood of Hyperactive Children," *Journal of Pediatrics*, 78: 985-990, June 1971.

[8]"Behavior Study Under Way," *EHLRI News*, 3: 1-5, September, 1973.

[9]Edward Ladd "Pills for Classroom Peace?" *Saturday Review*, 53: 66-68+, November 21, 1970.

[10]Laufer, *op. cit.*, p. 170.

[11]Randall Richard, "Drugs for Children — Miracle or Nightmare?" *Providence Sunday Journal*, Feb. 6, 1972, pp. 1+.

[12]*Ibid.*

[13]Helen F. Gofman, Bayard W. Allmond, Jr., "Learning and Language Disorders in Children," *Current Problems in Pediatrics*, 1: 3-60, September, 1971.

Chapter 8

✿✿✿✿✿ ✿✿✿✿✿ ✿✿✿ ✿✿ ✿✿✿✿

Birth Research

William Shockley and Arthur Jensen have achieved a good deal of notoriety because of statements which they have made in connection with the heredity versus environment issue. It is not the purpose of this chapter to agree or to disagree with Shockley and Jensen in this matter. If one wishes to examine the question as to what factor heredity and environment play in the development of I.Q., there are a number of sources[1] readily available. The purpose here is to show what is being done and what will be done in one area, that of genetic engineering, to produce brighter and healthier children.

In the United States, a nation with excellent hospital facilities, there are still a number of babies who die at birth or are born deformed or brain-damaged. Caputo and Mandell[2] have shown that low birth weight, as is found in cases of prematurity, is correlated with a number of deficits, e.g. intellectual impairment. Low birth weight is frequently found in the histories of mental retardates, individuals who have been institutionalized and High School dropouts. According to Caputo and Mandell, hyperkinesis, autism, and involvement in childhood accidents are also relatively common among prematures. These children also have difficulties in language development. Their physical growth, motor behavior, and neurological functioning are often adversely affected as well. One of the causes of prematurity is poor prenatal care, usually in the form of poor maternal nutrition.

The National Foundation-March of Dimes has warned women of the dangers of eating rare or raw meat or handling cat feces during pregnancy. The danger is from a parasitic infection — toxoplasmosis — which can damage the child's brain, cause blindness, or even kill the fetus. The National Foundation has estimated that five percent of the cases of blindness in this country are caused by toxoplasmosis. Research evidence suggests that *all* of these cases — regardless of the age at which they occur — might be the result of infection before birth.

Dr. John Ambrose, a government biochemist, has developed equipment which will make it possible for doctors to quickly check a new-born infant for a wide range of signs indicating various types of retardation. Adjustment of the child's diet can, in a number of cases, halt the retardation and allow the child to develop as a normal individual.

Because there are so many problems involved in the development and birth of an infant, much research is going on to determine how genetic defects may be eliminated.

Genetic abnormalities are of two types.[3] The first type results from the alteration of a single gene. This causes a number of diseases, such as hemophilia, muscular dystrophy, or cystic fibrosis, to mention but a few. These disorders would be correctible if each cell of an individual were given the appropriate genetic information. The second type of genetic abnormality results from an abnormality of chromosomal number or arrangement. These abnormalities are lumped together under the term "mongolism" and there seems to be no cure readily at hand.

Genetic evaluation of a fetus is now possible through amniocentesis. Amniocentesis involves the insertion of a thin, hollow needle into the amniotic sac and the withdrawal of a small amount of fluid. Analysis of the amniotic fluid can indicate genetic defects that are chemically evident but it does not indicate genetic defects that might be structurally visible.

Dr. Michael Kaback of the University of California, Los Angeles, is close to overcoming this problem. He has developed a scope about the same size as an amniocentesis needle that makes it possible to view a fetus. Dr. Kaback believes that it will be possible by using his scope to take tissue samples of a fetus and also to perform surgery on a fetus early in pregnancy. This could be a way of preventing a number of birth defects.

Another aspect of genetic engineering, reminding one of *1984*, is the possibility of in vitro fertilization, i.e. fertilization in a chemical solution in a glass tube. It is already possible to produce a human embryo in the laboratory by introducing male semen to a mature egg cell which has been removed from a female donor. Dr. Robert G. Edwards of Cambridge University in England has already grown embryos, fertilized in vitro, well beyond the sixteen celled stage. The embryos developed in this way can be studied microscopically to determine whether or not genetic defects are present. It is possible by means of in vitro fertilization and culturing of embryos to examine the earliest stages of human development as the egg splits into two, four, eight, and sixteen cells. It is at these stages that a number of genetic defects arise from the improper splitting of the chromosomes.

Dr. Edwards intends to introduce the embryo, after cell division has taken place about 100 times, into the womb of the female donor of the egg. There it would be allowed to develop and reach maturity. This technique has already been used to produce living mice as well as other animals. Dr. Edwards believes he will be able to produce a living human being in this manner within a year. Perhaps as you are reading this page you will have already heard of such a development. One thing that does not seem likely for some time yet is that a human baby will be born who did not need to be developed in the womb. The possibility of a nine month in vitro baby still seems to be many years away.

The importance of this work is that it will make it possible to observe and understand more clearly (1) the maturation of the egg through stages just preceding ovulation, (2) the fertilization of the egg, and (3) its development to the blastocyst stage.[4] By means of these observations, it should be possible to avoid certain causes of infertility and to prevent the development of embryos that could be expected to grow abnormally. (This last situation presents a moral issue to some which will be discussed later in the chapter). Two factors which might lead to abnormal development are damage to the egg cells as they are being handled or the possibility that an egg is defective to begin with. Many women who are seeking treatment

THE FUTURE: HUMAN ECOLOGY AND EDUCATION

FIGURE 8–1
THE FUTURE – DEVELOPMENT OF EMBRYOS IN VITRO

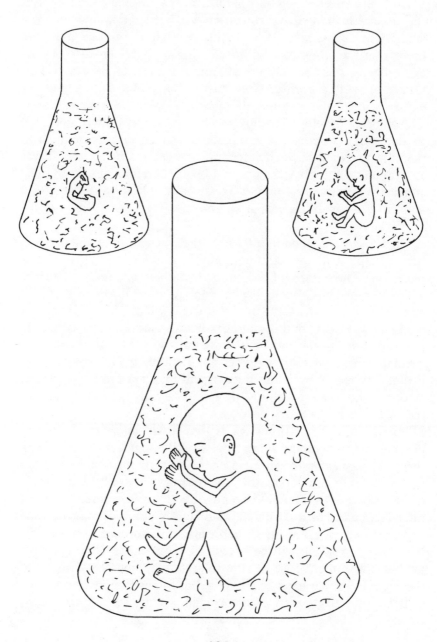

for sterility are in their thirties approaching the age of forty. The possibility of women in this age bracket producing a mongoloid child is much greater than for a younger woman. This is believed to be due to some defect in the egg cell. An advantage to in vitro fertilization would be that the parents would have selectivity in determining which embryo of several fertilized and developed eggs would be returned to the mother. The baby's sex could be predetermined in this way, and any embryos that were defective and could develop into a mongoloid child might not be of assistance to develop further.

A further advantage of in vitro fertilization is that the deeper understanding of early human development can be of assistance in developing new methods of contraception.

It would also be an advantage to families which carried sex-linked genes such as the one responsible for hemophilia to predetermine the sex of their children. The genes responsible for hemophilia are recessive and occur primarily in the male. If women who were carriers of this gene had only female embryos placed in their womb, the problem of hemophilia could be reduced. It would not be completely eliminated as 50 per cent of the female embryos would be carriers of the hemophilia gene. There has still not been a method developed by which it could be positively determined which of the female embryos carried the trait for hemophilia before they were implanted in the mother's womb. By means of amniocentesis the fetus could be typed to determine whether or not it carried the gene for hemophilia, but this could not be done until at least the fourth month of pregnancy.

Another advantage of in vitro fertilization is in cases where the woman produces mature eggs but the ducts linking the ovary and the uterus are blocked or missing. This situation occurs in about 25 per cent of all sterile women. Treatment will involve removing an egg, exposing it to sperm from the husband, and implanting the egg in the uterus once it is big enough to burrow into the uterine wall and develop there.

Advances have been made in the area of cloning. Cloning is the production of genetically identical copies of an organism. F.C. Steward,[5] a cellular physiologist at Cornell, has been successful in taking one individual cell from a carrot and bringing it to a full-grown carrot plant. This work, done in the early nineteen-sixties, showed that it was possible to grow a plant from an individual cell and, theoretically, to do the same thing with an animal cell.

John Gurdon, a biologist at Oxford, did this very thing with frogs' eggs. By using radiation, he destroyed the nucleus of egg cells without damaging the body of the eggs. He then took the nuclei from ordinary body cells of the frog and intruded them into the egg cells. The new cells were the equivalent of fertilized eggs, capable of producing adult frogs. Some of these cells divided to form normal tadpoles which developed into normal frogs identical genetically to the frog from which the nucleus was taken. Cloning had occurred using animal cells.

Before cloning can take place in human beings, there will need to be advances in the area of microsurgery and corresponding laboratory techniques. This is so because of the microscopic size of the human egg in comparision to the frog egg. The human egg is so small because it does not contain all the nutrient necessary to support the development of the embryo as is the case with the frog's egg.

Human cloning, which seems to be between 10 to 20 years off in the future, will be done in a partly similar way to the cloning of frogs. The nucleus of an egg cell will be destroyed and a nucleus from any cell of the person to be duplicated will be inserted into the egg by, as yet undeveloped, microsurgical techniques. The egg cells will be placed in a nutrient medium and cell division will take place. By the time division has reached the 8 to 32-cell stage, the egg will be ready for implantation either directly into the uterine wall at the proper time in the menstrual cycle or into the Fallopian tube where it would pass into the uterus and implant itself on the uterine wall.

Many people feel that cloning, once it is possible, could be used to produce duplicates of people according to predetermined specifications. We could have an athletic team made up of players cloned from a superstar or several superstars. We could produce clones from our political leaders, from the leading people in the arts and sciences, or from assembly line workers, or from the military. It would be possible to duplicate in quantity any individual for any purpose. It would also be possible by cloning to duplicate a loved one suffering from a terminal illness. As one can see there are certain advantages and also disadvantages to cloning.

BIRTH RESEARCH

FIGURE 8–2
THE PROCESS OF CLONING

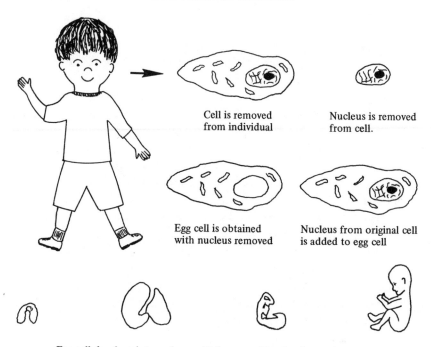

Cell is removed
from individual

Nucleus is removed
from cell.

Egg cell is obtained
with nucleus removed

Nucleus from original cell
is added to egg cell

Egg cell develops into embryo which grows either in vitro or in uterus

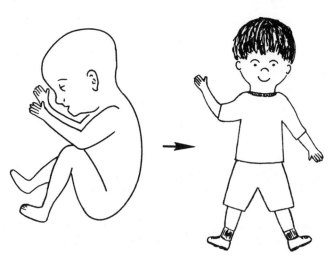

Embyro develops into genetically similar individual as one from whom original cell was taken

An individual, according to Gaylin,[6] is produced by interaction of his genetic variables with the environment. The individual can be altered by such factors as the cytoplasm of the egg, the biochemistry of the blood flowing through the placenta, and by the diet and emotions of the woman carrying the child. This is why the cloned individual could be so very different from the person from whom he was cloned. It is also possible that a cloned cell which genetically belongs to one woman could be developed in the uterus of another woman for nine months. This could happen in the case of a woman who was able to produce eggs but had some problem with her uterus. It also could occur in the case of a woman who was a professional worker and did not wish to go through the nine months of carrying the fetus in her womb. She could pay another woman to carry her child for the nine months. There is also the possibility of the development of an artificial placenta which would eliminate the need for the fetus to be carried in the uterus at all.

There are implications to be considered if we are to have fetuses developing in artificial wombs or wombs of women who are not the mothers of the children they will bear. We do not know for sure what effects maternal emotions have on the developing embryo. Would a woman carrying someone else's baby in her womb be as careful of her health as she would be if it were her own baby? We know that some expectant mothers smoke, use narcotics, and are poorly nourished. If this can happen even whey they are carrying their own children, what might happen if they are carrying someone else's child?

What will happen to those eggs that are not selected for further development in the womb? At what stage of development will they be abandoned? At what stage of development do these developing cells become children? Who will decide which embryos will be discarded and which will be allowed to develop? These are all questions which must be answered as we become more proficient in genetic engineering.

Cloning would be of great value in the area of animal husbandry. By cloning it would be possible to breed the best possible cattle for beef, or hogs for pork. We would have the ability to reproduce exactly those animals best bred for meat. In these days of soaring meat prices this would certainly be an advantage.

Cloning could also be used to prevent a species of animals or plants from becoming extinct. It would provide a simple method of building up the numbers of an endangered species.

It has been claimed that cloning and in vitro fertilization may be damaging to the self-concept of woman. This seems to be a male chauvinist idea based on the thought that the role of women is primarily that of becoming pregnant and bearing children. Many women have rejected this idea as the be-all and end-all of their existence and have turned to a number of other social roles. It seems that this is not as great a problem as what many men think it to be.

These advances in the knowledge of genetics have led to widespread genetic counseling services. A study, conducted by Dr. James L. Sorenson of Princeton, showed that genetic counseling could have an impact on a couple in the areas of personal identity, interpersonal relations, and social status as a family. However, many of the people receiving genetic counseling have difficulty in accepting genetic counseling information because the counseling very often involves an alteration of the self which is unacceptable to the person being counseled. The counseling is more apt to affect attitudes toward reproduction rather than actual reproduction behavior.

With the advent of genetic counseling, the question of the responsibility of society to regulate the response of families to counseling information must be considered. The question can arise as to whether the right to procreation can be restricted if there is a risk of bearing children with major genetic deficiencies? (Approximately one child in twenty is now said to be born with a discernible genetic defect.)

To answer this question one must consider the issues of free choice, the quality of life, the community of man, and the future of man himself.[7] Who is it who will decide what traits are desirable? What traits will be considered desirable? When will the decision be made? What will happen to those embryos which do not have all the desirable traits? Will they be discarded as just so much garbage or will they be allowed to develop? If they are not allowed to develop, what will happen to the diversity which exists among men? Will we be attempting to develop a super race along the lines of Hitler's plan? These are some of the questions which readily come to mind when one considers the area of genetic counseling. Answers to these questions can be given only in terms of what one's moral code or sense of right and wrong allows.

It is entirely possible that by means of genetic engineering we can eliminate the differences that exist between people. We could develop a race of people all with equal abilities. Is this desirable? What, if anything, will happen to that diversity which made America what it is today?

What are the implications for education if all the possibilities of genetic engineering are realized? The first implication would be that teachers would no longer be able to say that such-and-such a student could not read or learn this or that subject because he was retarded or incapable of learning unless he had had some accident after birth which led to retardation. We would have, as genetic engineering improved its techniques, students who would know more than their teachers.

We would have children who would not be content with schools as we know them now. These children would be capable of learning at an advanced rate. They would be capable not only of learning at a more advanced rate but would also be more capable in physical activities than their present-day counterparts. This would call for a new breed of teacher. There would no longer be a need for the teacher who feels that students cannot learn unless he, the teacher, is present. People, who have been developed through genetic engineering would be capable of a good deal of self-direction.

Advances, once they have been made, lead to still more advances. Progress occurs at a geometric rate, one advance leading to many others. This will be so in the field of genetic engineering. It will be impossible to predict just how far we will be able to go in this area, but, as of now, the work has just begun and the sky seems to be the limit.

1For further information on the heredity-environment question as it relates to intelligence, one might read the following:

Arthur Jensen. "How Much Can We Boost I.Q. and Scholastic Achievement?" *Harvard Educational Review*, (Winter, 1969), pp. 1-123.

Jerome S. Kagan, "Inadequate Evidence and Illogical Conclusions, *Harvard Educational Review,* (Spring, 1969), pp. 274-277.

J. McV. Hunt. "Has Compensatory Education Failed? Has It Been Attempted?" *Harvard Educational Review*, (Spring, 1969) pp. 278-300.

James F. Crow. "Genetic Theories and Influences: Comments on the Value of Diversity," *Harvard Educational Review*, (Spring 1969) pp. 301-109.

Carl Bereiter. "The Future of Individual Differences," *Harvard Educational Review*, (Spring, 1969) pp. 310-318.

David Elkind, "Piagetian and Psychometric Conceptions of Intelligence," *Harvard Educational Review*, (Spring, 1969) pp. 319-337.

Lee J. Cronbach. "Heredity, Environment, and Educational Policy," *Harvard Educational Review,* (Spring 1969) pp. 338-347.

William F. Braziell. "A Letter from the South," *Harvard Educational Review*, (Spring 1969), pp. 348-356.

Richard Herrnstein. "I.Q.," *Atlantic Monthly*, (Sept. 1971) pp. 43-64.

H. J. Eysenck. *The I.Q. Argument.* (Freeport, New York: The Library Press, 1971).

James S. Coleman, et al. *Equality of Educational Opportunity.* (Washington, D.C.: Department of Health, Education and Welfare, 1966).

Benjamin S. Bloom. *Stability and Change in Human Characteristics.* (New York: Wiley, 1964).

William Shockley. "Dysgenics, Geneticity, Raceology: A Challenge to the Intellectual Responsibility of Educators," *Phi Delta Kappan*, (January 1972), pp. 297-307.

N.L. Gage. "I.Q. Heritability, Race Differences, and Educational Research," *Phi Delta Kappan*, (January 1972), pp. 308-312.

2Daniel V. Caputo and Wallace Mandell "Consequences of Low Birth Weight," *Developmental Psychology*, 3: 363-383, 1970.

3"Genetics Advances Evoke Ethical Concern," *Chemical and Engineering News*, 51: 14-15, Jan. 8, 1973.

4R. G. Edwards and Ruth E. Fowler, "Human Embryos in the Laboratory," *Scientific American,* 223: 45-54, December 1970.

[5]Willard Gaylin, "We Have the Awful Knowledge to Make Exact Copies of Human Beings," *The New York Times Magazine,* (March 5, 1972), pp. 12-13+.

[6]*Ibid.*

[7]John V. Tunney and Meldon E. Levine, "Genetic Engineering," *Saturday Review of Science,* 55: 23-38, August 5, 1972.

Chapter 9

❧❧❧❧ ❧❧❧❧❧ ❧❧❧ ❧❧ ❧❧❧

A Look Ahead

To imagine the difficulty one has as he attempts to look ahead ten or twenty or thirty years all one has to do is go back a comparable period of time. Who in the year 1964, 1954, or 1944 could have predicted accurately all the events that are happening now? We are limited in predicting future events to a present day frame of reference.

Peter Drucker has stated the problem most accurately:

> All we can ever predict is continuity that extends yesterday's trends into tomorrow. What has already happened is the only thing that can be quantified. But these continuing trends, however important, are only one dimension of the future, only one aspect of reality. The most accurate quantitative prediction never predicts the truly important: the meaning of the facts and figures in the context of a different tomorrow.[1]

We know what yesterday's trends were. What we are not sure of are what the values and perceptions will be in the years to come. With the realization of these limitations we will now proceed to look at tomorrow in terms of today and yesterday and also in terms of the priorities envisioned as necessary for an orderly society.

129

THE FUTURE: HUMAN ECOLOGY AND EDUCATION

It is generally agreed that the earliest experiences people have, have a profound effect on their later behavior. Konrad Lorenz has experimented with goslings to show the effect of early experiences on their later life. In his experiments, Lorenz was the first living thing seen by newly hatched goslings. As a result, he was followed around by the goslings — a sort of father goose to the goslings. Similar results were obtained with other animals. The consistency of behavior demonstrated by the animals led Lorenz to his theory of "imprinting" which simply means that the early experiences in the life of animals determine their later social behavior. This theory has also received general acceptance in relation to man.

If one listens to Psychiatrists or reads books on Psychiatry, one sees that the most severe and damaging psychiatric harm has been inflicted almost always in infancy or early childhood. The results of this harm are evidenced later on as the person goes through life — a form of imprinting.

The imprinting can be changed by bringing about a new level of understanding. This can be accomplished with some difficulty through various methods such as meditation, biofeedback, drugs, or some traumatic incident.

Rather than have to change the imprinting, it would seem more advisable to present a "good" first imprinting which would not need to be changed. This is entirely within the realm of possibility. The first step for accomplishing this would be to use the knowledge available to geneticists now to see to it that birth defects were eliminated and that infants were given the best possible medical care, both pre-natal and post-natal, and that mothers-to-be and their babies received a proper, nutritious diet rich in protein. (These ideas were developed in chapters one, six and eight). In the years ahead we will see the elimination of a number of genetic defects. We will see a greater emphasis on proper pre-natal care and nutrition. We will see stronger, more intelligent babies because of in vitro growth of embryos and other genetic advances. In the near future it will be possible to develop nearly any type of individual desired by treating genes in such a way that desired characteristics can be realized. It may also be possible at some much later time to develop a complete replica of an individual by the process of cloning.

It could be possible in the near future for a woman to shop for the kind of baby she wants. She could select one embryo from a number

A LOOK AHEAD

FIGURE 9-1
METHODS OF CHANGING IMPRINTING

Meditation

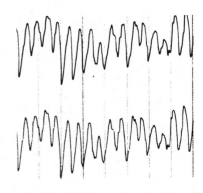

Biofeedback — Alpha Rhythm

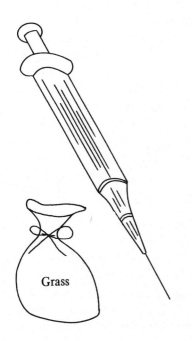

Grass

Drugs

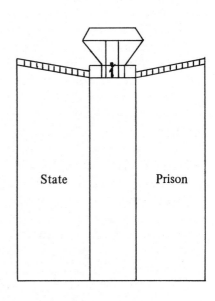

State   Prison

Trauma

of available ones which would be labelled as to sex, color of eyes, color of hair, probable size and I.Q. The embryo implanted in the woman's womb would develop there for nine months. The embryo would also be guaranteed to be free of any genetic defects.

Dr. James Bronner, a professor at the California Institute of Technology, has suggested that within two or three generations we will be mass-producing super babies which will become "the saviours of mankind" which will soon fall prey to what he calls natural evolutionary forces and like any other species, decline toward extinction. He feels that committees will be set up to select donors of sperm and ova which will be frozen and then placed in host mothers who will bear the children. The donors would be selected, according to Bronner, on the basis of still to be drawn guidelines. The ethical and moral questions presented by such a proposal are obvious and not easily solvable if we wish to preserve individual freedom. We may in the future need to decide just how much of our freedom we are willing to give up, if any, to produce these so-called "saviours of mankind."

Babies will be tested shortly after their birth. This testing will continue on a regular basis as the children grow to see to it that their physical and mental development proceeds as it should.

In the future schools, in cooperation with the social agencies and the medical experts in a community, will help to instruct parents on how to do a better job of raising their children. Parents will be taught to understand the outcomes of their actions, as well as alternative methods of reacting to their children. They will be taught the importance of talking to their children from the day they are born. Parents will also be taught to provide stimulation for their babies in the form of moving, brightly colored objects which the baby can reach for and touch while he is in his crib, of sound stimulation through music, and the like.

Neurological testing will be an integral part of pediatric checkups. This testing will be used to identify infants who are in need of neurological treatment — treatment which if administered early enough can cure the condition in a number of cases.

With this type of care and training the imprinting should be good and a number of problems of society can thus be reduced. Schools will work more closely with parents and the community and will begin to work with parents and their children within a few months of their birth.

FIGURE 9–2
THE FUTURE – EMBRYOS FOR SALE?

Special Sale
Money Back Guarantee
Save BIG!!!
Satisfaction Guaranteed

We Accept All Major Credit Cards

Children in the primary grades will be taught through the process of biofeedback to control much of their autonomic system. They will learn ways of altering their consciousness through meditation. In the future, people will not have to rely on alcohol, sleeping pills, stimulants, depressants, tranquilizers, or other drugs to get them through the day. They will be able to exert control over themselves and get the effect of a changed state of consciousness simply by willing it to happen.

For those children who continue to have problems, counseling services will be expanded. Presently there are a few isolated communities or medical centers which offer complete pregnancy counseling and abortion services for a growing number of girls between the ages of eleven and seventeen. These services will be expanded to other communities in the years ahead. They will also be expanded to include counseling in the areas of drug and alcohol abuse, suicide prevention, venereal disease, psychiatric problems of runaways and other troubled teenagers, marriage counseling, and the routine health needs of adolescents. The realization that adolescents are prone to adult social problems will give impetus to this form of counseling.

One of the problems that can arise from such a counseling service is that the data on such adolescents can be fed into computers. Already this is true in a number of cases, even if only for credit card billing purposes. At the present time, personal information and medical diagnoses of 15,000 Massachusetts mental health patients as well as patients from other New England States, has been fed into a computer bank at the Rockland State Hospital in Orangeburg, New York. While access is restricted to each state's own data and there are legal and technical safeguards for confidentiality, such information storage could be potentially harmful to the rights of citizens. With the emphasis on computer storage of information, there can be a potential harm to the individual rights of privacy, to doctor-patient confidentiality, and to the rights of juveniles to be protected against public disclosure as guaranteed by both State and Federal laws. There is and will continue to be danger in participating in information systems that can reveal confidential patient information which is supposed to be protected by law.

But there are a number of benefits which will come from computer data banks. Information retrieval systems will play an ever expanding role in the future in the area of diagnosis of both psychiatric and physiological problems. *Index Medicus* provides diagnostic computer help for doctors at the present time. In the future even more doctors will take advantage of it to help in the diagnosis of their patients. Information stored in a computer can analyze electrocardiograms and electroencephalograms sent directly over telephone lines. In the near future these and expanded services will be available to every doctor in his own office through a telephone line which is hooked up directly to a computer.

There will be an attempt to improve the human condition in the years ahead. As children are taught early in their lives to alter their consciousness they will be able to become genuinely interested in and concerned for their fellow human beings. There will be an attempt to alter the living conditions both in isolated rural areas and crowded city slums. In both situations there is an abnormally high incidence of mental retardation as well as an unusually high rate of malnutrition, illness, unsanitary conditions, inadequate housing, accidents, lack of health care and education, apathy and poverty.

All of these conditions are interrelated with the result being a self-perpetuating cycle of poverty. For this cycle to be broken the social, economic, health, educational, and political systems will need to work together. This will necessitate the formation of day care centers where infants and young children would be left and would receive educational, health, and nutritional services while their parents were being re-trained or re-educated or educated to become self-sufficient members of a community.

With the present day emphasis on ecology, it will be an easy and natural step to become involved in the area of human ecology. We will see this emphasis on the ecology of the environment being balanced with an equal emphasis on the ecology of the human being.

Human development teams, which will include people in medicine, nutrition, psychology, sociology, and education, will be formed to work in rural or urban areas with about fifty families each. These teams will serve as a kind of ombudsman for the families they service to see to it that these families receive a diet rich in protein, that they have decent housing, and that they receive the type of education which will allow them not just to survive, but to thrive in the years ahead.

Presently there is a good deal of emphasis on the concept of "career education." The concept is good but the implementation is usually not so good. "Career education," if it exists in the elementary grades in a school system, usually takes the form of a teacher telling children about various occupations (usually in a sex-role orientation, e.g. Boys grow up to be men who are doctors, lawyers, policemen, firemen, etc. and girls grow up to be women who can be housewives, nurses, teachers, secretaries, etc. Not too many teachers (female ones included) tell their female students that they can also grow up to be doctors, politicians, policewomen, etc.) or having people who work at different jobs visit the class to tell the children about the kind of work they do.

At the junior high and high school level the student, as a part of "career education," is placed in some type of job situation for part of the day. The unfortunate part of this is that there is difficulty finding enough job situations for all the students who wish to participate in this type of program (or who wish to escape from school a few hours earlier each day) with the result that a number of students are placed in menial jobs. They end up not wanting to pursue the particular career they find themselves in and when they try to find a better job they discover that their education is not really adequate for any other position. In short they have neither the career nor the education to improve their situation.

According to Peter Drucker:

> . . . we will have to replace today's "vocational training" by the education of technologists. This will have to be "general" education, indeed in the true sense a "liberal" education. It should be a cornerstone of tomorrow's education for everybody.
>
> Equally important is the training and formation of perception and emotion in school. This is needed however we conceive the ends of education. The trained perception and the disciplined emotion are as pertinent to the ability to earn a livelihood as they are to the mature human personality. They are man, above all . . .[2]

In the era of human ecology ahead, if we wish people to thrive, we cannot attempt to train them for a single position. We must provide them with an education in which they are taught basic skills upon which they can build. In the era of human ecology emphasis will be placed on the basic skills of reading, writing, and arithmetic, as well as on the training and formation of perception and emotion, mentioned by Drucker. Human ecology, by its very nature, requires that people attain basic skills. It will be one requirement of the human development team to see to it that all family members they are servicing acquire the ability to read. The result will be that, in the future, we will not be graduating people from high school with only a fifth or sixth grade level reading ability. Everyone, in the era of human ecology, will be equipped with the basic skills which will allow them to thrive. They will also have learned how to learn out of necessity. This necessity is due to the rate at which knowledge is growing.

Alvin Toffler has stated that

> . . . by the time the child born today graduates from college, the amount of knowledge in the world will be four times as great. By the time that same child is fifty years old, it will be thirty-two times as great, and 97 per cent of everything known in the world will have been learned since the time he was born.[3]

Whether this learning will have to take place in the school in the future is questionable. Why is it necessary to transport children from a number of locations in the community to a centrally located school? In this day and age and in the future it is possible and it will become even easier to transport knowledge to students rather than having to transport students to a knowledge center — the school.

We have the technological know-how to educate children in their homes now. As this know-how is refined its cost will be lowered to a reasonable rate. This future education will be accomplished by having each home in a community equipped with a computer terminal giving both adults and children access to a number of programs of study. Another aspect of future education in the home will be the greatly increased number of educational television channels and a corresponding raising of the level of the quality of educational television. A third phase of this educational program of the future would involve providing each family with a microfiche reader and a supply of reading materials on microfiche.

THE FUTURE: HUMAN ECOLOGY AND EDUCATION

What would happen to school teachers in the future if this type of education were initiated? Very probably we would need fewer teachers and those who did remain as teachers would be responsible for developing logical programs in their subject areas as well as for the diagnosis and treatment of students who had some form of learning disorder. This role is not different, or at least it should not be different, from the role of teachers at the present time.

The student of the future will learn to relax and expand his mental awareness through a process of meditation. Transcendental meditation is one such systematic procedure of

> . . . turning the attention inwards towards the subtler levels of a thought until the mind transcends the experience of the subtlest state of the thought and arrives at the source of the thought. This expands the conscious mind and at the same time brings it in contact with the creative intelligence that gives rise to every thought.[4]

Transcendental meditation, which is practiced for a few minutes in the morning and evening as one sits with eyes closed, has been found to significantly decrease oxygen consumption, carbon dioxide elimination, cardiac output, and heart and respiratory rate. It is apparent that, during transcendental meditation, the individual gains a profoundly deep state of rest while the mind remains awake and able to respond to stimuli. Studies of the blood of meditators have shown a reduction in the level of lactates in the blood during and after meditation. It is believed that anxiety symptoms are correlated with high blood lactate levels.

Among the benefits of transcendental meditation for the individual and for society would be the reduction of anxiety, the reduction of drug abuse because the student could alter his own consciousness without resorting to chemical means, and an improved attitude and behavior on the part of the individual. Another benefit would be in the area of increased learning ability because of the improved attitude toward learning on the part of an individual involved with transcendental meditation.

Meditation and biofeedback training (see chapter four) will be an integral part of the education process of the future. Not only students but also teachers and administrators will undergo training in either meditation or biofeedback or both. People will learn to control their bodies, their emotions, and moods in the school of the future.

RNA, DNA, or protein, in the form of pills will prove to be most beneficial in the future in helping people to learn. Direct chemical and electrical stimulation of the brain should also help to improve the learning process in the future. Hypnosis will also be used as a tool to enhance the learning process. Children in the future will be taught to develop their extrasensory perception (ESP). ESP refers to information that is not received through the usual senses and includes telepathy and clairvoyance.

The doubts that people have about the existence of ESP will gradually disappear and we will, in the future, come to understand how ESP operates and how it may be practically applied. We will come to a greater realization of the benefits which ESP can provide in developing the creativity and potential of each individual.

A number of people seem to possess ESP to varying degrees. We have all probably experienced the sensation of going to the telephone to call a friend or relative only to have the phone ring and, upon picking it up, we find that it is the person whom we are going to call. It seems that the person we were going to call thought of us as we were thinking of him. This could be classified as a low-level form of ESP. At a higher level we have the individual who can pick up an envelope and tell what is written on a piece of folded paper inside the envelope. Other individuals, when blindfolded, are able to correctly indicate the colors on a card simply by touching them. These are all examples of forms of ESP.

A still higher form of ESP is reputed to exist. This form involves the ability of doctors and other individuals to diagnose patients based on energy fields surrounding them.[5]

Victor Adamenko, a Russian physicist, has been working with a device which he claims takes pictures of the "bioplasmic energy" of animate or inanimate objects. The device is an electrical Tesla coil which is connected to two metallic plates. The object to be pictured, as well as a piece of film, are placed between the plates. A high-energy frequency is generated by turning on the switch. This frequency then causes the film to record a glow surrounding the object. Flare patterns are obvious in pictures of human heads and hands. There appear to be streams of light coming from both areas when pictures are taken in this manner. According to Adamenko the flare patterns change quite rapidly if the individual is hypnotized, drinks alcohol, or takes drugs.[6]

As more is found out about ESP, this process will be applied to bring about tremendous advances in the field of medicine. It appears that many people do have a potential for ESP. Education in the future will enable man to utilize that potential in such a way never thought possible. The potential of ESP is remarkable.

In the education of the future there will no longer be the emphasis on I.Q., grades, and grouping. Everyone will learn on an individual basis so there will be no need for grouping (if we still have schools). With individualized instruction each student will complete one unit before going on to another one. The testing will be such that if a student does not pass the test for a particular unit he will simply go back and take it over after some study or remedial work until he does pass it.

While few will mourn the passing of the emphasis on I.Q., which has been considered unfair to economically disadvantaged people, there is a method for measuring I.Q. which does eliminate this bias. If I.Q.'s are used in the future they will most likely be evoked potential I.Q.s.

John Ertl[7] has developed a method of measuring a person's I.Q. based on evoked potentials. The method indicates a high degree of relationship between the electrical activity of the brain and intelligence as measured by psychological tests.

Evoked potentials are non-random changes in the electrical activity of the brain in response to sensory stimulation. This electrical activity is indicated by means of an electroencephalogram (EEG).

If a stimulus is presented to an individual, his brain will always respond at approximately the same time after the stimulus was presented. An early response is one which usually occurs in less than one-tenth of a second and a late response is one which occurs after one-tenth of a second. The response of the brain (evoked potentials) to light and sound stimuli speeds up as the child grows older, is fairly constant in adulthood, and then slows down in old age.

According to Ertl, the rate of the evoked potential is related to information processing in the brain. Ertl has hypothesized that evoked potentials are the electrical signs of information processing in the brain and that it is, therefore, reasonable to postulate that the efficiency of the process may be related to human intelligence.

Ertl tested his hypothesis with 100 subjects between the ages of 18 to 50. These people were given the Otis I.Q. test. The I.Q. scores ranged from 77 to above 136. Evoked potentials were then determined for each subject by measuring the times which it took for each one's brain to respond to 100 light flashes. The tests of Ertl indicated that there was a high correlation between a high I.Q. score and a quick reaction time as indicated by an evoked potential of less than one-tenth of a second. Experiments have also shown that there is a good deal of difficulty in producing a change in the evoked potential pattern of an individual. According to Ertl, the concept of measuring I.Q.s by means of evoked potentials could produce significant changes in educating children. These changes may be directed toward maximizing the potential of each individual by using sensory inputs leading to the most efficient areas or by trying to improve less efficient areas. Measurement of I.Q.s by evoked potentials should help to diagnose a number of learning disabilities and could also help in the determination of which people could receive the most benefit from remedial educational programs.

Such programs will be of tremendous help in eliminating some of the social problems which exist today. It has been found that a large number of children, referred to authorities as juvenile delinquents, have reading problems and are reading well below grade level. If the I.Q. were to be measured as Ertl has proposed, it would be possible to determine which children could benefit most from remedial or developmental reading programs and initiate such programs for them.

In the medical area, much work is presently being done which will lead to remarkable advances in the future. One such development is the possibility that electrical signals might be applied directly to the visual cortex of the brain using a number of very small radio transmitters and receivers arranged in a grid so that a very crude picture of the outside world could be presented spatially on the cortex, without having a large number of wires passing through the skull. It is very likely that in the future blind people will be able to see by means of radio signals which will produce a picture by cortical stimulation.

THE FUTURE: HUMAN ECOLOGY AND EDUCATION

There are at present a number of artificial parts which can be implanted in the human body. These include such parts as the heart, arteries, joints in fingers, wrists, elbows, shoulders and artificial devices to replace larynxes, tracheas, and ureters. There is a good deal of controversy about the possibility of scientists ever creating an artificial brain. Some people believe that it is altogether possible while others feel that an artificial brain would be impossible to develop. It does seem that with the increased knowledge of the functioning of the brain it will be possible at some time in the future to produce an artificial brain or to transplant a brain from one person to another. Whether such a brain, either artificial or transplanted, would be desirable is open to question. What is certain for the future is that there will continue to be groups and individuals who will raise questions about the ethical problems which will be created by such advances in the sciences and medicine.

An example of the type of ethical problem faced in the field of medicine is the right of researchers to experiment on aborted fetuses. What right does the researcher have to experiment on aborted human fetuses even if the research is aimed primarily at developing artificial methods of keeping very early premature babies alive until they can survive on their own? What if the aborted fetuses servive long enough to be on their own? What then happens to the unwanted fetus? What rights does the fetus have? In the area of psychosurgery, as mentioned earlier, a Michigan court has ruled that experimental brain surgery to change behavior could not be performed on persons confined against their will in institutions. There are still a number of questions that need to be answered in the field of medical research.

That there have been abuses in the area of medical experimentation seems obvious. In the Tuskegee syphilis study a number of men suffering from syphilis were left untreated so that the natural history of the disease could be studied. In another instance, mentally retarded teen-age girls were sterilized without the informed consent of either the girls or their parents.

The ethical issues in the cases of experimentation on aborted fetuses, psychosurgery, sterilization, and studies which do not attempt to cure an infection are complex. The problem of preventing abuses in the future will become even more complex. As a result, it is likely that in the near future we will see the establishment of a board or commission for the protection of people subjected to bio-medical research.

One of the ethical issues faced by doctors and the relatives of a dying person is the question of how much outside help should be given to merely postpone an inevitable death. Doctors and relatives are becoming more aware that it is not necessary to sustain life for an individual who has no hope for survival, and that in some cases it is more humane to all concerned to withdraw a life-sustaining system than to maintain it. In the future, as we learn still more about artificial organs and as we learn to delay the aging process, this ethical issue will become even more complex. Should a life-sustaining system be withdrawn if it is possible to transplant or substitute with artificial ones more than 50 percent of the individual's organs, including his brain to insure him an even chance at survival?

While the Fountain of Youth sought by Ponce de Leon may never be attained, it does seem likely that within the near future we will achieve some control over the aging process. Current research with animals indicates that their life-span can be increased greatly by such techniques as reducing food intake, by lowering body temperature, or by introducing various chemicals into the diet. Further research is taking place with the idea of finding what it is within the cells that determines how many times they will divide. It is possible that once the genetic code for aging in man has been determined we will be able to greatly increase his life-span, by altering his genetic code. Success in the area of an increased life-span will lead to a future which will be concerned with new population control efforts.

A field in which relatively little research has been done is the area of deferred dying. Dr. David P. Phillips, a sociologist at New York State University at Stony Brook has been studying the phenomenon of deferred dying. Phillips has found that the death rate for a large number of famous Americans declined during the month immediately preceding their birthdays. The death rate was 17 percent lower than would be predicted by chance. The death rate among these famous Americans rose by 11 per cent during the three months following their birthday.

Phillips has found that the same lowering of the death rate has preceded every presidential election in the United States during the

143

twentieth century. Why such a phenomenon occurs is not evident, but if it were possible to determine what it is, whether chemical or psychological, which causes the deferral of death, we might be able to help people learn to live longer lives.

Studies show that up to 80 per cent of serious physical illnesses develop when a person feels helpless and alone. The death rate for widows and widowers is 10 times higher in the year following the loss of their spouse than for other people their age. Divorced persons, in the year following divorce have an illness rate 12 times higher than married persons of a similar age. These figures seem to indicate that as a person undergoes stress he is more likely to become ill and the more stress undergone, the more serious the illness is likely to be.

Dr. Thomas H. Holmes, a psychiatrist at the University of Washington School of Medicine, has devised a social readjustment rating scale which lists 43 events associated with varying amounts of disruption in a person's life. Each event on the scale was given a relative stress value. (See Table 9-1).

According to Dr. Holmes, an accumulation of 200 or more points on the stress scale could be more stress than a person could withstand during the course of a year. Such an accumulation of stress points could very well make an individual susceptible to disease. People who are able to withstand major disruptions in their life pattern seem to have no pre-existing susceptibility to illness. It is very likely that in the future we will develop an educational process that will teach people a greater control of their own system, emotions, and moods. By doing this it will be possible to teach people to greatly reduce stress-induced illnesses in the future.

As we look to the future it appears we will use the knowledge of bio-rhythm to help us become aware of the dangers we might face because our biological time clock is out of synchronization. A growing number of scientists are beginning to accept the idea that bio-rhythm charts, based on the date and time of one's birth, can be drawn up. These charts indicate on what days a person is likely to be accident-prone or subject to illness.

The Flight Safety Foundation, in 1971, sent out a newsletter about the human factor as it related to accidents and discussed the bio-rhythm theory of accident causation. The Foundation, in its newsletter, used as an example a Japanese transportation company

A LOOK AHEAD

TABLE 9–1
THE STRESS OF ADJUSTING TO CHANGE*

Events	Scale of Impact
Death of Spouse	100
Divorce	73
Marital separation	65
Jail term	63
Death of close family member	63
Personal injury or illness	53
Marriage	50
Fired at work	47
Marital reconciliation	45
Retirement	45
Change in health of family member	44
Pregnancy	40
Sex difficulties	39
Gain of new family member	39
Business readjustment	39
Change in financial status	38
Death of a close friend	37
Change to different line of work	36
Change in number of arguments with spouse	35
Mortgage over $10,000	31
Foreclosure of mortgage or loan	30
Change in responsibilities at work	29
Son or daughter leaving home	29
Trouble with in-laws	29

TABLE 9—1 (Continued)
THE STRESS OF ADJUSTING TO CHANGE*

Events	Scale of Impact
Outstanding personal achievement	28
Wife begins or stops work.	26
Begin or end school	25
Change in living conditions	25
Revision of personal habits	24
Trouble with boss.	23
Change in work hours or conditions	20
Change in residence	20
Change in schools	20
Change in recreation	19
Change in church activities	19
Change in social activities	18
Mortgage or loan less than $10,000	17
Change in sleeping habits	16
Change in number of family get-togethers	15
Change in eating habits	15
Vacation	13
Christmas	12
Minor violations of the law	11

*From Jane E. Brody, "Doctors Study treating of Ills Brought on by Stress,"
The New York Times, Sunday, June 10, 1973, p.20.

which operated a railroad and a fleet of 700 buses and taxis. This company has applied the theory of bio-rhythm to its operations. In the first year of charting bio-rhythms for each employee, drivers were reminded to be extra safe on the days that appeared critical on their bio-rhythm charts. The result was that the company's accident rate decreased by one-third while the accident rate in Japan, as a whole rose steeply.

The future will see greater attention paid to the cycles which people go through with bio-rhythm charts to indicate dangerous times. We will learn not only to cope with stress when it is presented, but also to avoid times and situations which can be extremely stressful because of our knowledge of bio-rhythm.

Most people are familiar with the process of photosynthesis, in which green plants produce food and give off oxygen in the presence of light.

Because of the awareness that light is important to man and all living organisms an interest in the study of photobiology has developed. Photobiology is the study of how visible light interacts with living cells. Impetus for the study of photobiology has come from John Ott and the Environmental Health and Light Research Institute.

Ott first became interested in photobiology while taking time-lapse pictures of pumpkin plants growing and flowering. He found that under cool white fluorescent light only male blossoms developed. When these lights burned out and were accidentally replaced by daylight white fluorescent lighting, only female blossoms developed. In further time-lapse photography experiments with apple blossoms, Ott found that apples would not turn red if they were grown in such a way that ordinary glass came between sunlight and the apples.

Experiments such as these with plants soon led to further experimentation with animals. Chinchilla breeders prefer breeding arrangements that produce a preponderance of females rather than male chinchillas. This is so because one male can service a number of females in the breeding process, producing more females which in turn produce more of the valuable chinchillas. Ott found that under normal incandescent lighting chinchillas produced almost all male offspring. When the lighting was changed to a bluish color, almost all of the offspring were female.

147

In other experimentation with time-lapse photography of fish eggs Ott found that the type of light used on aquariums was responsible for determining the sexual development of the fish. When pink light was used on the aquarium, 80 percent of the fish which hatched out were female.

Similar experiments were performed on mice and again the results indicated that the type of lighting which was present had an effect on what happened to the mice.

Another form of experimentation began when Ott accidentally broke his glasses. After breaking his glasses Ott found that an arthritic condition in his hip started to improve and eventually disappeared. He also found that his vision began to improve without the glasses. For the first time in a number of years, according to Ott, his eyes were receiving ultraviolet light. It is Ott's opinion that a form of photosynthesis occurs in animals. Ott explains:

> In the retina of the eye are special cells - known as pigment epithelial cells - which apparently have nothing to do with vision. I've found that such cells from the eyes of rabbits react abnormally when deprived of particular wavelengths of light.
>
> These pigment epithelial cells seem to stimulate the pituitary and pineal glands inside the skull by exciting certain nerve pathways. These glands in turn control the endoctrine glands which produce and release hormones - substances which affect growth, fertility, emotions and the body's ability to resist many diseases.8

Research is currently underway at Loyola University's Stritch School of Medicine to learn how light impulses are transmitted from pigment epithelial cells to the endocrine system. It appears that it will take several years before the answer is found.

To back up his contention that light is important to good health Ott, in 1959, provided instructions on exposure to natural light to 15 cancer patients at the Bellevue Medical Center in New York. After following Ott's instructions for the summer, it was found that in fourteen of the patients tumor growth had stopped and several patients seemed to be improving. The one patient, whose tumor had not stopped growing had misunderstood Ott's directions and had continued to wear ordinary eyeglasses which filtered out the ultraviolet rays in the sunlight.

Russian and Swedish scientists have found that they can reduce the number of colds caught by factory and office workers by adding ultra-violet waves to the light environment of their offices and factories.

Other experimentation by Dr. Irving Geller, Chairman of the Department of Experimental Pharmacology at Southwest Foundation for Research and Education in San Antonio, has shown the effects of abnormal conditions of light and darkness on the pineal gland of rats. The pineal gland is one of the master glands of the endocrine system. Geller has found that under stress rats prefer water to alcohol until left in continuous darkness for extended periods. When left in continuous darkness the rats preferred the alcohol. The reason for this might be learned from earlier experiments performed by Dr. Julian Axlerod. In these experiments it was found that during dark periods the pineal gland produces more of an enzyme - melatonin - than during light periods. When melatonin is injected into rats who are on a regular light/dark schedule these rats become alcoholic.

It may be possible by means of such knowledge to cut down or eliminate the problem of alcoholism completely. If it is found that the pineal gland in the human being, by producing too much melatonin, is responsible for the condition of alcoholism, it should be possible to suppress the production of melatonin either by light or chemical means and elminate the problem of alcoholism.

As mentioned earlier in chapter seven Ott has concluded from experimentation that classroom lighting can be a factor in causing hyperactivity in children. It appears that a good deal more research must be performed to determine just what effect light has on the pineal gland. This is a new frontier which holds a great deal of promise for the future.

In a totally different area, we will in the near future learn to communicate with animals and understand what they are "saying" back to us. The U.S. Navy's Undersea Research and Development Center at Point Loma, California, has trained porpoises to detect enemy mines and frogmen, to retrieve military hardware from the ocean, to rescue frogmen, and to protect divers from sharks. It has been suggested that the Navy has developed a "man to dolphin" translator that transforms human speech into pitch modulated whistles understood by the porpoises. This report has not been confirmed but it is probable that if such a device has not yet been developed, it will be. The procedures used in developing it could be applied to similar translators to be used with certain other animals.

It is likely that before the end of this century we will also have found proof of the existence of intelligent life on other planets and established contact with these beings. Computers should help to develop codes that could be used for such communication.

These are but a few of the many changes which lie ahead for us. We have a chance to revolutionize the educational process and the human condition chemically, medically, biologically, and technologically. We are indeed on the verge of a brave new world, a world of tremendous opportunity for all.

---

[1]Peter F. Drucker, *The Age of Discontinuity*. (New York: Harper & Row, 1969), p. XII.

[2]*Ibid.* pp. 318-319.

[3]Alvin Toffler, *Future Shock*. (New York: Random House, 1970), p. 141.

[4]Maharishi Mahesh Yogi, *Maharishi Mahesh Yogi on the Bhagavad-Gita: A New Translation and Commentary* (Baltimore: Penguin Books, 1969), p. 470.

[5]Shafica Karagulla, *Breakthrough to Creativity*. (Los Angeles: DeVerss & Co., 1967).

[6]Stanley Krippner and Richard Davidson, "Parapsychology in the U.S.S.R.," *Saturday Review*. pp. 57-60, March 18, 1972.

[7]John P. Ertl, "Evoked Potentials and Intelligence," *Revue de l'Universite d' Ottawa*. 36 (4): 599-607, Octobre-Decembre, 1966.

[8]George Lepesky, "Does Indoor-man Need Outdoor Light?" *Midwest Magazine*. pp. 34-39, November 4, 1973.

For additional information the reader might refer to:

Lewis M. Andrews and Marvin Karlins, *Requiem for Democracy?* (New York: Holt, Rinehart and Winston, 1971).

A LOOK AHEAD

Arthur B. Brenwell (editor), *Science and Technology in the World of the Future*. (New York: Wiley-Interscience, 1970).

Wayne O. Evans and Nathan S. Kline, editors, *Psychotropic Drugs in the Year 2000*. (Springfield, Ill.: Charles C. Thomas, Publisher, 1971).

Dennis Gabor, *The Mature Society*. (New York: Praeger Publishers, 1972).

D. S. Halacy, Jr. *Genetic Revolution*. (New York: Harper & Row, 1974).

Richard Kostelanetz, *Human Alternatives*. (New York: William Morrow and Company, Inc., 1971).

George B. Leonard, *Education and Ecstasy*. (New York: Delacorte Press, 1968).

George B. Leonard, *The Transformation*. (New York: Delacorte Press, 1972).

John Ott, *My Ivory Cellar*. (Chicago: Twentieth Century Press, Inc., 1958).

Jean Rostand, *Humanly Possible*. (translated by Lowell Bair) (New York: Saturday Review Press, 1973).

Alan F. Westin, Michael A. Baker, *Databanks in a Free Society*. (New York: Quadrangle Books, 1972).

Jerome J. Wolken, *Photobiology*. (New York: Reinhold Book Corporation, 1968).

Index

ACKNOWLEDGEMENTS

The preparation of this book has truly been a family effort. My thanks go to my wife Rose and to Mrs. Mary Kelley for their work in typing the manuscript.

Special acknowledgement also goes to my wife Rose, not only for her work in typing and proof-reading the manuscript, but also for her encouragement, support and patience during the time this book was being written.

Thanks also to Helen Sullivan and to Linda Saia for their assistance in proof-reading and to my older children, Eddie and Paul, for their help in preparing the index.